❧ Some ❧
Instructions

Some
Instructions
Stanley Crawford

JONATHAN CAPE
THIRTY BEDFORD SQUARE LONDON

First published in Great Britain 1978
Copyright © 1978 by Stanley Crawford

Jonathan Cape Ltd, 30 Bedford Square, London WC1

British Library Cataloguing in Publication Data

Crawford, Stanley Gottlieb
Some instructions.
1. American wit and humor
I. Title
818'.5408   PN6162
ISBN 0-224-01622-9

Printed litho in Great Britain
by W & J Mackay Ltd, Chatham

To Dennis Jarrett

Portions of this work were written
under a grant from the
Literature Program of
the National Endowment for the Arts.

She is my goods, my chattels; she is my house,
My household stuff, my field, my barn,
My horse, my ox, my ass, my any thing.

Some
Instructions
*To My Wife Concerning
the Upkeep of the
House and Marriage,
and to My Son and
Daughter Concerning
the Conduct
of Their Childhood*

 Contents

CONTENTS

CONTENTS

FOURTH AND LASTLY · *To My Wife Concerning
Some Final Dispositions*

THE MARRIAGE ALMANAC · 155

INDEX · 169

First

To My Wife Concerning the Upkeep of the House and Marriage

1 ❧ Putting Things Away.

Keep all things clean and keep them put away in their proper places, whereof you know, and take them out when needed and, when used, put them back into their places, whether they be cupboards, shelves, cabinets, boxes, sacks or bags, or the yellow or green trash containers under the sink; the ones made of plastic.

2 ❧ Friends Near and Far.

When the women of the neighborhood wish to tell you of their sheets and bedding, turn a deaf ear, though it is permissible to listen if they live sufficient distances away, over a hundred miles away, for example, so that daily intercourse is not likely, and therefore it does not matter to me what they do, they and their husbands, between the sheets, and I will not have to lend either of them money, tools, seed, or grain, or advice, or help start their cars, repair their stovepipes, or move their freezers. For knowledge is power, my dear, and power diminishes in proportion to its ultimate destination or administration in time and place, its terminus; far friends, as we know, are good friends, while with near friends one must live with deaf ears, although with friends both far and near it is perhaps best and wisest to be deaf while they are near and keen of ear when they are far, and both when they are in transit from the one state to the other.

3 ❧ Daily Appearances. Your seemingly interminable training will be complete when the appearance of each room of the house corresponds to its appearance for a set hour of the day, each day, for a set period of weeks, months, years—whatever. To make this clear, let us take an example. Supposing there is a cloud of dust in the living room—it is being swept, vacuumed, dusted, repaired—at four in the afternoon, then at every subsequent four in the afternoon there should appear a like or similar cloud of dust raised by a similar process, as generated by a like or similar person dressed in a like or similar manner employing approximately the same gestures to achieve the same end, a cloud of dust.

4 ❦ Running Lists. The keeping of a running list of household needs is, my dear, essential to the smooth operation of the entire house, and I cannot easily overemphasize the importance of it, however much I might try and try. For what could be more disastrous to the even temper of the household than to wake up one fine morning and discover snow piled halfway up to the roof and no sugar left in the kitchen—no butter in the refrigerator—no toilet paper in the bathroom? Thus a good rule is to make note of an item when it is two-thirds or three-fourths depleted, that is, when three out of four quarters of butter have been eaten, three out of four rolls of toilet paper used up, or six and two-thirds pounds of a ten-pound bag of sugar emptied. You may also find it useful to lay in a reserve of essential items for emergencies, as long as you make a note to replenish those that are used up during such emergencies as may have come to pass so that should emergencies recur there will always be emergency supplies from which to draw—for there is nothing worse than to discover in an emergency that the household is not only out of regular supplies but out of emergency supplies as well.

The keeping of a list is not, however, as simple as it may first seem, for it is not enough to start at the top of the page and write out the items in the order in which they come to mind, that is, in an order in which their exhaustion draws near. Certainly one must start in this fashion, but this is not to say that you should finish here, with a randomly drawn-up list that corresponds to no order except that of chance. It is for this reason that I have posted in the pantry a floor plan of the supermarket at which we habitually shop, and with the most important items marked and labeled according to aisle and counter. Now of course I cannot guarantee the daily accuracy of this map—for unscrupulous supermarket operators are likely to scramble everything up overnight in order to confuse and bewilder their customers into buying their way out of the labyrinth—but I do take notes on the latest changes every time we shop so that I may then revise the map the moment we return home, as I think you have often noticed.

Thus I suggest that the mornings we set aside to go into town to shop you get up especially early in order to re-cast your first rough draft of a list into an order that corresponds to the path I have recommended you take through the supermarket, that is, starting from the right of the building, fresh produce, and threading your way through the aisles, up one and down the next, until you reach the left side of the building, the meat counter, and from thence pass directly to the checkout stalls. In this way the whole circuit can be completed in ten minutes or less and will not expose you to undue or prolonged temptations, while allowing me sufficient time to inspect the aisles and counters for changes or alterations of any sort.

Nor should you fail, upon returning home, to enter all items purchased, both separately and as totals, into the housekeeping account book I have provided for your exclusive use, and then to balance these totals against the cash contents of your purse and my wallet in relation to the original sums we first left the house in possession of or withdrew from the bank on the way. In this manner you can easily spot any miscalculations you may have missed earlier, notably overpricings, which may be brought to the attention of the supermarket manager the next visit into town, or any pure and simple losses, while accounting also by the same means for all coins or bills found on the sidewalks or in the parking lots or elsewhere, behind cushions or under chairs. In any case, whether we go shopping or not, it is a good idea to make certain twice daily, once in the morning, once in the evening, that such cash as we carry about with us is flowing through the course of the day without secret losses, which, if left undetected, could mount up to considerable sums over the years.

5 🎗 Inventory Lists. To know the contents of the house is also to know the contents of the Marriage, not only the large but the small as well, from major appliances and furniture down to handkerchiefs and doilies or even pins and needles, and it is for this reason that I have prepared an inventory list for your use in keeping up the house. Needless to say, you should carry it around with you at all times so that you can use it to verify the correct number and condition of our possessions and thus be able to discover almost at once when something is lost—disappears—is stolen—which is more likely to happen with the smaller objects of the household than with the larger. Nonetheless you will find it useful as you walk into the kitchen each day to ask, consulting your list, whether there are the right number of stoves, refrigerators, tables and chairs in the room and if not, why not, or, if they are all there as they should be, whether any of them is in need of repairs or maintenance or total replacement. In this way the condition of each object of the household can be ascertained by a glance at the list (without having to rummage through everything), and replacements can be ordered and purchased in advance, before the sheets rip or the towels fray or the shirts give out at the elbows, thus avoiding ill-timed failures, whether of garment or of appliance. And it is a task best carried out in the early morning hours of each day—as you may gather from observing me go over the yard and garden each morning with my inventory list in hand, noting down the condition of the trees, shrubs, fenceposts, walls, gates, livestock, garden rows, tools and supplies, car and truck, and whatever else might

have been damaged by the passage of time or the weather or carried away in the darkness of the night.

6 ❧ Household Calendars. The

function of the household calendar, that is, the various schedules I myself draw up for our joint use for the year in progress, is to assure that the days flow smoothly one after another in such a way as to spare either you or me, the joint partners of the Marriage, the sort of surprise or shock that can be occasioned by abrupt and unannounced changes. Health is a function of diet and regularity, and that is why I have made a point of marking down not only the hours at which I wish all meals to be served over the course of the year, but also a detailed menu for each meal, each day of the year—the menu and meal hours schedule I keep posted on the inside of the pantry door. You will note slight seasonal variations in both hour and menu content which are keyed—you might also notice—to slight variations in the hours I have set for going to bed and getting up in the morning, which are in turn reflected in the time and length of the afternoon nap. There are also minor variations tied to the phases of the moon. What is unpredictable here is the weather—yet I have attempted to make allowances, particularly for those days and weeks it is most likely to be extreme or abnormal. And the eating and sleeping schedules are also reflected in the dressing schedule to be found posted inside the clothes closet and on which I have indicated what articles of clothing I will wear for each day of the year, in turn mirrored in the seasonal bath and shower schedule, the whole indicating— if you read between the lines—those nights I have scheduled in advance for going out to be entertained or for other extraordinary activities, as listed on the schedule pasted to the inside of the glove-box door of the car. The utility of this system should by now be obvious to you, for should we find ourselves fully dressed up at five in the afternoon —having dutifully followed the bathing and dressing calendars—then it should be clear that this is a night to go out and that we should then proceed to do so, following as closely as possible the itinerary suggested inside the glove-box door, to Chinese or Italian restaurant, foreign or domestic comedy, chamber music or symphonic concert, and so on, whenever the facilities and activities in the neighboring towns permit, as usually they will.

The whole, of course, composes what I often refer to as our Marriage Almanac, on the composition of whose various calendars and schedules I spend at least three whole evenings each year, that is, the year preceding its actual issuance. For I have often observed that a Marriage will most often founder on the little matters of when and what to eat, what to wear and when to wash or clean it, when to go out and where to go and when to stay home, when to invite someone in and who it should be, and so on, and thus to follow the Almanac of our Marriage is to avoid making these decisions on the spur of the moment—since I have already made them months in advance, from an objective distance in time when I am neither hungry nor thirsty nor affected by the weather, hot or cold, nor can have any idea of what films or plays or concerts might be scheduled for the neighboring towns, and am thus best able to determine the shape and form, as it were, of the upcoming year, down to its most seemingly insignificant details. And further, by publishing my little Almanac—as I intend to do someday, in the distant future—and mailing copies to our friends, we will not only be able to inform them in advance of our schedule for each day of the year, thus sparing us unwanted or inconvenient visits, but provide as well a model of sorts upon which they may wish to reconstruct their own Marriages in order to reinforce and strengthen them.

7 🎋 The House.

The house is the Marriage, and thus to maintain and keep in good repair the house, tidy and well cleaned, is to keep the Marriage too in good repair, tidy, well cleaned. The house, with its four walls, roof, floor, windows and doors, resembles the Marriage in other respects as well, so that if you focus your attention on the house you are focusing your attention on the Marriage as well. Many well-known proverbs come to mind here, all proven by time beyond memory, and I am content to let them stand as they are. In substance they state that it is the duty of the Wife to keep the interior of the house clean (as was said) as well as to offer food, drink, clothing, and bedding to those who enter its doors, that is, the invited, while it is the duty of the Husband, who I happen to be in this case, to keep the exterior surface of the house in good repair so that there will be no leaks, drafts, darkness where light is wanted, light where darkness is wanted, nor any intruders of any sort through any of the openings in the fabric which composes the outer walls. Yet if you fail to see me at these tasks, unremitting as they easily can be, guarding the ramparts, so to speak, oiling the locks on the doors, checking the tightness of the bars across the windows, scanning the horizon with my telescope—then do not suppose me gone. I am always around.

8 🐾 The Yard.

As the house is the Marriage, so too can the yard or grounds or the land be seen to represent what came before the Marriage, and by that I mean the courtship, for a house can no more be built on thin air or on a cloud in the sky than can a Marriage begin without an introduction and subsequent courtship. Thus as the house needs its lot or land to sit on, so does the Marriage need its courtship, its romance, or its affair to sit on also beforehand. And in the same way neither is the house nor the Marriage simply dropped from the sky onto the land without any preparation whatsoever, to fall wherever it may. Certain things must be investigated beforehand by the prospective Husband and Wife before building their house, which is also their Marriage. In the first place, the fiancés should study their lot or land to make certain it is well drained and that its subsoil is such that it will be able to support the vast weight of the foundation and structure of their future house. Then they should decide where the house will be best situated in relation to scenic views and neighboring roads or highways, prevailing winds and breezes, and the course of the sun across the sky, supposing that they are wise in the choice of their site to begin with, and are well out of sight of neighboring houses, stores, factories, highways, and railway lines. Next they will have to arrange for the thickets of wild rose and plum and willow or whatever other wild vegetation there might happen to be growing to be bulldozed off into a corner and burned, for how else will they be able to build their house if the growth upon their property is rank and tangled? With their land cleared and naked of vegetation, they may order the digging of the trenches for the foundation and the pipes, and command that wires be brought down from the sky to deliver their electricity. They will watch the walls rising next—the walls which must be strong. Beams will be hoisted. The roof will be nailed on, tarred, graveled, and it must not leak. Then the plastering will begin inside the house to make the walls smooth and true, not only along the vertical but along the horizontal as well. The strong doors and tight windows go in, and the sleek drapery, and the rich carpets that are nailed down to the floors. A van arrives with the bridal furniture and appliances and the nuptial bedding. Finally the fiancés, now Bride and Groom, arrive with their honeymoon suitcases and trunks and move into their new house.

And as they lock the doors behind themselves and begin taking up residence in the house, so too do they begin taking up residence in the Marriage itself, which, like the house, has been built upon land stripped of all vegetation. Thus at first as the Bride and Groom look out the windows they will see only desolation and loneliness on all sides— all that remains of their once flowering courtship. For as the house and thus the Marriage are built and moved into, so too is the land and thus the courtship laid waste to, the one growing out of and consuming the other and thus bringing about a momentary ecological imbalance. But this is as it should be, for to prolong the courtship in the interests of preserving the flora and fauna of the land, so as not to disturb the mounds of red ants or cut back the poison ivy, is to postpone the building of the house and thus the Marriage in the mistaken belief that the courtship can last forever, in plain defiance of the laws of nature. Autumn and winter follow upon spring and summer, whereupon the once admired wild roses lose first their blossoms, then their leaves, then their hips—while the house stands upright, eternal, or relatively eternal—eternal enough, at any rate—and sheds the snow with its peaked roof and remains inside like spring and summer through the heating action of stoves and furnaces. And over the years the house asserts itself and comes to preside over the land upon which it stands, surrounding itself with well-trimmed lawns and well-planted flower beds in the place of the former growth which was wild and undisciplined. So too, then, should the Marriage work at replanting the devastated land of the courtship, not only with lawns and orchards, but with easily cared-for annuals and perennials as well, whose blooms are both predictable and regular throughout the various seasons of the year.

9 ✌ The Roof.

As the Marriage is the house, so the roof of the house is the roof of the Marriage, that is, what keeps the Wife and Husband dry. The importance of keeping dry, my dear, is well understood, and it is my earnest wish that you keep the objects of our household dry and in good condition against the time when they will have to be used. Tight containers are excellent for this purpose, from plastic bags to waterproof trunks, and can serve equally well to keep certain objects that should be kept wet, wet or moist. The floors should be dry except when being cleaned, when they may be wet for brief periods of time, or when wet by accident (as in the dropping of bottles), as long as they are returned to a condition of dryness as soon as possible so that sticky substances are not tracked throughout the house. As the roof of the house keeps out the wet (rain, snow, etc.) from the house, so too does the roof of the Marriage keep the wet out of the Marriage. You should think of the roof of the Marriage as a kind of lid.

10 ✺ The Floor.

Likewise the floor of the house can be considered the floor of the Marriage, that is, what the Husband and Wife stand on and walk on and what they rest the furniture on. As is well known, floors are both dirty and "clean" at the same time. Yet it can also be said that no floor is ever entirely clean so much as it is "not dirty" or "not very dirty." But it is an agreed-upon principle that the floors of the household are to be kept as clean as possible and that this is primarily your task and that you should furthermore guard against dirt being tracked into the house and therefore into the Marriage. And should you perform your duties in this area in the proper manner, it follows that you will not have to worry about dirt being tracked out of the house, out (therefore) of the Marriage.

11 🖎 The Walls.

The walls of the house represent the walls of the Marriage, and as one or two walls standing alone represent a ruin, so do four or more walls in multiples thereof represent the closing in upon, the rounding out of, the consummation of the copulatory embrace, though vertical rather than horizontal. The house then represents the sexual act frozen into architecture, and though doors will open and slam closed as children run in and out, and windows will be flung open in summer and latched closed in winter, and faucets be turned on and toilets flushed, and fires lit and be allowed to die out—we cannot ignore this fact. Therefore as you make your rounds throughout the house in the course of the day, cleaning the floors, walls, ceilings, and other interior surfaces (while I am at work outside rehanging shingles, touching up cracks in the plaster, repainting the trim), it would be well to consider where you are. For as the interior of the house (and we also mean by "house" Marriage) is the female and what is outside the house is male, it follows that whenever I (who am the male) enter the house, which lies passive and horizontal and open unto my comings and goings, and as I wander among its furnishings (which we will call the organs), the overstuffed armchair, the pink sofa, the rich red carpets, and come upon you, surprising you and—but what more is there to add?

12 ❦ Electricity.

The modern house with all its conveniences can no more function without electricity than can the modern Marriage function without its equivalent, and by that I mean the nervous energy which powers the Marriage. For the wiring of the house with its wires, outlets, and switches is also the wiring of the Marriage or the nerves of the Marriage through which electrical impulses are transmitted, causing light bulbs to glow, toasters to heat up, the motors of washing machines, blenders, and other appliances to turn, and so on. And as the electrical circuits should not be overloaded by turning on all the lights and appliances at once all over the house, so too should not the wiring of the Marriage be overloaded by putting too many demands on it at once if one is to avoid overheated lines and blown fuses. For the effect of the blown fuse is to plunge everything into darkness and make time stop. Yet this can sometimes happen accidentally, as when the Husband and the Wife are drawing power in large quantities from separate ends of the house unbeknownst to each other. In such cases either you or I but preferably both of us should immediately undertake to find candles and flashlights and go down into the basement and replace the fuse or reset the circuit breaker, and start all over again. But now and then the lights will go out unexpectedly in the middle of dinner, the result of a distant lightning bolt, for example, and there is nothing that either of us can do except to sit quietly by the candles until the lights finally go back on. That is, there are two kinds of power failure within the Marriage, the one brought on from within, the other from without; the effect, however, is essentially identical.

13 🦋 Hospitality.

As you know, my dear, I now and then forsake the house to stand in the bushes for longer or shorter periods of time, except when it is raining, but that does not mean that I have removed from my view the houses of others, which people the landscape on all sides. But neither do I, the male, visit much anymore these other houses, for my duty is to guard my own house above all, to stand at the threshold or down at the gate, where I must keep myself stronger than the whole world, however insignificant I may appear to be elsewhere, among a crowd, say, or proceeding down a highway in a small car. And should—to give you some advice—someone come to the door of the house and ask to be admitted, supposing he is a male, admit him certainly—hospitality demands it—but ask that he wipe his feet and that he sit in the hard chair near the window, and ask him what he wants within the first few minutes of his visit and then tell him, the moment he has finished his coffee, the moment you hear a soft banging coming from outside, where it is, outside, that he wants to borrow.

14 ❦ Textures.

As materials of various textures will cover the interior surfaces of the house, so will the interior of the Marriage be covered or upholstered in a variety of ways. I speak broadly here and mean not only the fabric that covers the frames, springs, and padding of furniture but include as well carpets and drapery and wall coverings, if other than plaster and paint, and countertop materials. To a certain extent the room of the house will dictate the type of texture to be found in it. You will notice that the living room is essentially "woolly." The textures in it are rough and fluffy, as in the deep-pile carpet and the shaggy upholstery of the sofa and armchairs, and in the drapery. This is intended to convey an impression of warmth—as the guest steps into the room it is as if he is being offered a blanket or towel or some other covering. So too the upholstery of the Marriage, that is, the various fabrics which serve to conceal in a decorative and pleasing manner the wooden frames and springs of the furniture of the Marriage as well as to bind it all together and make it more durable.

It should be clear, however, that what may be pleasing to the eye and comfortable to the body in the living room or bedroom will not be so in the kitchen and the bathroom, where what is wanted is the hard gleaming surface that wipes up well, does not chip, scratch, or stain—what in fact can hardly be called upholstery at all. Yet the principle is the same or similar, for the smooth slippery surfaces one finds in these rooms serve to speed the work that is to be done in them, such as washing, cooking, dishwashing, just as the woolly surfaces of the other rooms inhibit thoughts of speed and slipperiness and can easily bring on drowsiness and sleep. But the main point is that as you make your rounds of the house in the morning according to the schedule I have recommended to you—the one I have posted inside the broom closet—it is important to distinguish these various textures one from the other and so clean them accordingly, and not mix everything up into the neither rough nor smooth that is passed over lightly with a duster and thus called "clean." Woolly textures must be vacuumed daily with our powerful machine and the dust bag emptied after each use in the incinerator in the backyard, except when the wind is blowing, and slippery surfaces must be scrubbed with a brush and sponge every day, using a pail of water (warm is best) into which has been added the correct amount of the appropriate disinfectant. It should be clear that it is best not to confuse either the two types of textures or the two methods of cleaning them. The same, of course, may be said of the Marriage as well.

And you should take special care as you move about the house cleaning it not to leave more traces of yourself as you are cleaning it up than you are in fact cleaning up, for the fewer traces of either the Wife or the Husband the cleaner and more tidy and well kept is the Marriage itself. The perfectly kept house, as you know, is one in which there appears to be no one living and in which the laws of physics, chemistry, and biology seem to have fallen into suspension, for here is a space that has been fastidiously isolated from the more ordinary universe—it is a space in which things do not crumble and fall, liquids do not spill or splash, fabrics do not fade or tear, glass does not crack or break, paint peel, wood discolor, tiles stain, hair fall out

—it is a space into which the visitor will peer as into a museum case where the daily implements of a long-vanished race are carefully arranged. Such is the ideal you might consider striving for, unattainable as it may seem at first glance.

15 ❧ The Houses of Others.

As the house is the Marriage, so you will learn as you enter and come out of the houses of others, going in the front door and coming out the back, and vice versa, the condition of the Marriages. Is the house shapely from a distance, for one, and unified and compact, or is it an ill-harmonizing mélange of styles? Is it in good repair, with solid floors and thick walls and a tight roof, or is it made of flimsy materials that cause it to be hot in summer and drafty in winter, or both, with terrible alternations—in spring and autumn? Was it built by the occupants or did they merely buy it and move in, or are they only renters, here today and gone tomorrow? Many of these things you will be able to see from afar, whether on foot or driving, while most will require examination from close range. Look at the doors. Are they well hung or do they bind? Look at the windows. Are the panes cracked and is the putty falling out? Is the glass clean? Look at the upholstery of the furnishings, if there are furnishings, if they are upholstered. Carpets—if any. Plumbing: it is a surprisingly easy matter to go through a house in the presence of even a large family and check out the plumbing without anyone being entirely aware of the fact, to include hot and cold water taps at all sinks, the toilets and whether they flush properly or "run" all the time, baths, showers, washtubs—an activity that lends itself well to being combined with checking out the wiring, whether all switches work, all electrical appliances singly and in combination with others without blowing a fuse or tripping the circuit breaker—and depending on the season you will receive a fairly good idea in the course of these inspections of to what extent the heating and air-conditioning systems of the household work, that is, how well or badly, without even asking. And finally, are the occupants of the house happy with the house—do they appear to be happy when they say they are —or are they obviously exhausted by thirty or forty years of living in a drafty house with weak wiring and constricted plumbing and ready to move out at the drop of a hat—and so on. These and many other tests can be made, and with them you will know, when you come to say goodbye and leave the house and its occupants, you will know the condition of the Marriage, whether it is sound or not, well or poorly maintained, tidy, filthy, stuffy, drafty, and so on.

Yet that is not all. For in approaching and coming away from the house you will have occasion to notice the conditions of the yard and garden, that is, the land upon which the house as well as the Marriage is built. Is the garden contented and flourishing and weedless, or is it worried and fretful, its plants growing in a spindly manner from earth packed hard—or is it merely a beautiful vision born of a warm spring day and now vanishing among the weeds of midsummer? Are there bald patches in the lawn where dogs roll? Have the trees been trimmed so that you can walk under them freely, and pruned of dead branches and excess growth? Do birds sing in them or are they infested with cats lying across the branches, twitching their tails? So also with the animals of the barnyard, toward which you should make a little detour in order to inspect their condition, to see whether the hens appear contented and are lorded over by a suitably important rooster or are lethargic and scruffy, with tails plucked out and feet swollen, and the rooster croaking timidly in a corner while lifting now one foot, now another—whether the pelts of

FIRST • *To My Wife*

the doe-goats are sleek and glossy in summer or thickly
furry in winter with no bald patches indicating worms or
worse, their hooves trimmed, their udders large and full,
their bite true, their eyes alert—and the buck in the next
pen, whether he chortles with desire, extending and re-
tracting his organ and irrigating the fence—or lies quies-
cent in a corner, his manger filled with brown and moldy
hay; and so also, in a similar manner, with cows and
cattle, rabbits, ducks, geese, and whatever other domestic
animals there happen to be, for where the animals of the
Marriage are contented, well fed and well housed, so too
is the Marriage itself likely to be contented and well fed,
its pelt glossy, its plumage in good repair.

16 ❧ Clothes.

If the house is the Marriage, then the clothes that the Husband and the Wife wear are the words that bind together the Marriage, the vows or vowels and consonants. The clothes or clothing must be kept clean at all times (if the Marriage is to be a good one) and washed whenever necessary to keep them in that condition of cleanliness, and by clothes I mean under and outer garments of all kinds, including socks or stockings, handkerchiefs, hats, gloves—but mainly referring to pants or trousers, skirts, dresses, shirts, sweaters, and the like. They are to be washed, furthermore, in the laundry room, which was constructed especially for that purpose and, on clear sunny days, are to be taken outside and hung on the line until dry, where they will benefit from the sterilizing effects of ultraviolet rays from the sun, whereupon they are to be brought back into the house and folded or ironed and folded and put away in their proper drawers, closets, chests, and hampers, whose existence I have spoken to you of many a time, and where they can be easily found, unfolded, put on, worn until soiled—and so on. Now as the house is the Marriage and as the clothes are the vows, so do the clothes hang upon the Bride and Bridegroom and by them they shall be known—not, however, necessarily to each other. For clothes hang upon the Husband and the Wife like the foliage on the trees, and from them are to be known the species and the genus—whether tree, bush, shrub, flower, edible vegetable, weed, as well as the season, by which I mean the time of year. From this can be seen that the vows represent an intention while the language that follows, in Marriage, represents the foliage through which the path of life wends its way and from which one plucks fruit, leaf, flower, or seed, including the cotton boll from which is made clothing. But the main point is that, with clothing, we clothe our nakedness, retain the warmth of our bodies in the cold of winter, and encourage a shading-cum-ventilation process in the heat of the summer. Could not the same, then, be said of the vows?

But I am not finished with this matter either. For when in the Marriage the clothes are not washed and dried according to the general indications above, then they become soiled and offensive to others, can cause sores and infections, and ultimately must be discarded—having passed the stage, as happens so easily, where they can ever be washed perfectly clean again.

17 ✺ Doors.

I have spoken on windows and doors, but not absolutely. For it is through the door that comes the neighbor bearing fragrant packets of gossip still warm from the oven, as well as the friend who comes to hear, the relative from afar to listen. The door or doors, then, represent the mouth or mouth and ears of the Marriage through which enters matter of various sorts including sound waves from the world outside the Marriage, and as Wife of the house and thus of the Marriage you are advised to let this matter pass through you in a manner both speedy and traceless, for the strength of the Marriage is being tested each time you hear the screen door opening or the telephone ringing. You have observed the goats and how they will rub for years at a section of the fence they suspect to be weak (but will not see in their dimness that it is the strongest section of all) until after a period of years the nails loosen, the boards split, and the fence clatters to the ground: so do friends and relations come in and out of the doors of the house until finally the house, the Marriage, collapses upon the heads of the Husband and the Wife, as we have seen so many times, as weakened by the cumulative effects of sound waves and other vibrations.

18 ✤ Windows. But whereas the doors represent breaches in the fabric of the Marriage, that is, the house, the windows are altogether another matter, representing the eyes, for they are bastions of strength despite their apparent fragility. The windows should be kept clean at all times, first of all for the simple pleasure of being able to look through them and, conversely, for the displeasure to be found in staring at films of smoke or rainsplashed dust, the droppings of insects on the interior surfaces of the glass and those of birds on the exterior surfaces, for it may be said that a house with clean windows is a Marriage with clean eyes, that is, eyes that see clearly. Curtains, shades, and blinds are to be drawn or lowered at night, however, so that the outside world in its prowlings around will not be able to see inside the Marriage and what goes on or (in some cases) what does not go on, and they are to be drawn open or raised promptly at the first light of dawn so that there is no doubt that the house is alert and awake as early as it is convenient to be so. Likewise lights are to be turned off inside the house promptly at eleven, since late nights—as in the Marriage's flashing eyes—suggest discord or argumentation between the Husband and the Wife, and should this prove necessary, should the Husband and the Wife choose to quarrel after eleven at night, they are advised to draw the curtains and lower the blinds and turn off the lights and to quarrel in a low voice, a whisper if at all possible. The curtains, shades, or blinds represent the eyelids of the Marriage, it should be pointed out.

The windows are one of the more complex structures of the house and consist of glass (as was mentioned), mullions of metal or of wood milled and lap-jointed, putty, and in some cases hinges and latches, that is, for windows that open and close, and paint or stain inside and out. They may also be weather-stripped in the case of windows designed to open and close, or merely caulked in those windows that will remain fixed for all time. Windows may also be covered at various seasons by screens, awnings, storm windows, all for various reasons—suggesting the sunglasses, hat brims, etc., of the Marriage. But windows are in all characterized by a quality which is of supreme advantage to those, the Husband and the Wife, who jointly inhabit the house, and that is that one obtains a better view looking out of windows from inside than looking in through them from outside, an effect which is enhanced by the quadri-focal bi-stereoscopic vision innate to the Marriage itself, as summed up in the saying: two can see better than one. Thus not only can one see better from within looking outward, not only that—there is also the matter of simply being inside while the objects or persons outside are outside, for inside one can communicate in low tones without fear of being overheard, while outside one is not only bi-stereoscopically visible but subject to certain unexpected resonating configurations in the shrubbery, fences, and walls that can serve to project one's softest words right into the house, and in this effect lies the supreme strength of the Marriage over others, who know not how much they are being watched, how much overheard.

19 ❧ The Weather.

There is one other effect of doors and windows which I have failed to mention, and this is to keep out the weather. The same of course may be said of the walls and roof of the house, which prevent the entrance of rain, snow, hail, and wind, whether blowing hot or cold. But no house will be completely free of the effects of the weather, for there will always be windows and doors that leak water when a wind blows the rain straight against the house or when snow piles up outside the doors overnight, and the interior of the house will grow hot or cold in accordance with what is going on outside at most any time. And here, in these changes, is an ideal topic of conversation between Husband and Wife, for the weather is something that can often be both vague and precise, certain and uncertain, pleasant and unpleasant, useful and useless, and thus is a subject that can never be truly exhausted and about which never enough can be said. No doubt you have noticed my preference for it above all other subjects. What drama lies in the air around us! Thus you would do well to learn a little more about the high- and low-pressure fronts that cross and recross the skies above our house, and to study the manner in which storms can arrive early, on time, or late, or how they can vanish without a trace, and the way in which temperatures will rise toward the afternoon and fall toward the morning. It is also useful to note the effects of rain or snow or frost or hail not only upon the crops in the garden but upon the parts of the body sensitive to changes both gradual and abrupt, such as skin, muscles, and joints. From these observations lively subjects of conversation can be readily worked up to decorate the silence of the house—but need not be limited to only what is commonly called the weather. What is the condition of the sun today?—I may ask. Bright? Middling? Weak? Or, was the moon in good form last night? The stars? Twinkling? Dim? Obscure? Recent signs of intelligent life? And so on, to give you some idea of the kind of question I may choose to ask about the weather, either at the end of the day, over dinner, or at the very beginning, over breakfast.

And as the weather may be said to be the tangible effects of the heavens upon the movement of various air currents in the sky and the way they interact with day and night and humid and dry masses of air and clouds of minuscule particles, so too may the weather of the household, which is the weather of the Marriage, be said to represent the tangible effects of movements of masses of cold or hot air, humid or dry, such as the coughs, sneezes, colds and fevers, plus other storms of the Marriage as generated by the Husband and the Wife, from which signs various predictions and forecasts can be made concerning the weather that is yet to come. And the weather of the Marriage, like that of the sky, is something that must be watched closely at all times, for it is only the careless and unobservant who lose crops to the spring frost or see their woodpiles disappear under the snow—having left them improvidentially uncovered—or fail to sandbag their fields against the flood. Thus you would do well to keep a sharp eye out for those early signs that indicate the coming of sudden storms, and against which you should lay in stores, cover what is uncovered, and prepare yourself in any other way that you possibly can.

20 ❧ Fires.

Regarding fires, furnaces, heaters, and incinerators, all of which the modern house will be equipped with, as is our house, a few remarks. I have pointed out the necessity of keeping combustible matter —paper, oil-soaked rags, cans or bottles of paint, kerosene, turpentine, and so on—away from these appliances, and in the case of the fireplaces to keep the flues clean particularly during extremely cold weather in order to guard against the buildup of soot and creosote, which can result in a fire in the flue. Now the function of these appliances, as you know well, is to heat the house during the winter, with the exception of the incinerator, more of which later perhaps, and though they are not normally used during the summer when it is hot they are still "active"—that is, their pilots continue to burn nonetheless, unless they too have been shut off. Now as the house is the Marriage, so these devices fueled by natural gas, wood, coal, and electricity represent the basic passion that keeps the house, the Marriage, warm during the cold months— this is the flame that drew us together to warm our hands and feet on that dark, moonless beach some years ago: the night was bitterly cold and the sand very damp, that much I remember. The importance of keeping these fires going throughout the winter is therefore obvious, for without them the house becomes uninhabitable at the worst or the inhabitants become grouchy and irritable, as you will notice when you visit the houses of those stingy with their fires as compared to those who keep great logs blazing in their fireplaces at all times and their thermostats turned up high and who wear light clothing. But it is equally important to note that the fuel, whether gas, electricity, coal, or wood, to feed the flames that warm the house must in general come from afar, at considerable expense and effort —somebody's effort (the householder himself, where the fuel is wood gathered nearby), particularly if the house is large and of many rooms—that is, if the passion is large that fuels the marriage. Economics and finances are therefore factors. The worst case is probably that of the large, drafty house heated by many fires of different kinds, or ill heated, that is, ill fueled by a weak and impoverished passion. An average case would be that of a Marriage heated by one energy source as financed by an average income of passion but subject to increasingly unstable market conditions as time goes on. A good case might be one of a well-insulated house requiring little heat of any kind to keep it warm and in which logs will be burned in a fireplace during the snowy nights for a kind of decorative effect, not heat. And there have been known to be cases in which the fueling of the house required an effort so great as to leave no time to sit in front of the fire and enjoy its effects, not to speak of cases in which the house was too evenly heated day and night, or cooled, thus lulling the inhabitants into a state of torpor.

And so as you and I lie together at night in our bed we are like the logs that nestle together in the fireplace, and it is my work to light the fire in the evening by means of paper and kindling, to blow on the flames with my lips or with the wheezy action of the bellows, though it is the work of either of us or both to empty the ashes when the hearth is full to overflowing, as is the work of keeping the firescreen well placed in front of the flames so that sparks do not fly out and burn a hole in the carpet or ignite it, which could lead to the burning down of the whole house—and by that I mean the Marriage.

21 🦢 The Children.

As you know, my dear, I have taken it upon myself to limit the number of our Children to two, one Son and one Daughter, the greater part of whose care I entrust to your apparently sound maternal instincts. There is thus little I can offer by way of advice or recommendation except to say that I do not wish to meet them more than once or twice a day and preferably toward the end of the day and preferably at that part of the end of the day when they are being put to bed, which is also near the hour I have at last managed to dismiss most of the greater concerns of the day and thus am able to summon up the strength to once again introduce myself as their Father. They are, at this time in their lives when they are particularly subject to beneficial influences—I am pleased to note—learning. It would help of course if you would refer to me regularly throughout the day by pointing to me through the windows as I work out in the yard or as I get in the car and drive away, or as I pass close by the house on the way to get a tool from the garage or return one I have finished with. In such manner they will become accustomed to viewing me at various angles and distances, and in various postures, or moving now slowly, now rapidly, on foot or by car. You may now and then—but perhaps no more than once a day—wish to carry them out in your arms so that they may have a close view of me in direct sunlight—or, as one of them seems to be walking after a fashion, send him for a brief ramble down to the garden walls and let him (or her) peer through the cracks in the gate, staring and blinking, before you call him (or her) back. And when they are old enough to speak in complete sentences and thus to understand them when spoken to them, you might consider reading them aloud, once a day or so, selections from some of my published horticultural pamphlets, particularly *Garlic Questions Finally Answered* and *How to Garden Without Bending Over.* These things must not be hurried, however. There is plenty of time for the Children to get to know me, and I see no reason why they should be rushed into the matter when all of life is yet ahead of them.

Although we will have no more Children—we already have 0.3 too many as it is, statistically speaking—it may nonetheless be said that every day lived within the house, thus within the Marriage, is one of utmost pregnancy. For as you go about your way within the house cleaning and dusting, washing clothes and dishes, and I go about my way outside making repairs and tending the yard and garden, we bear within ourselves, the Husband and the Wife, images or effigies of each other, the Husband of the Wife, the Wife of the Husband, and carry these images about with us as we work. And as the pregnant mother-to-be will have no clear idea of what her future child will look like, or how it will behave, imagine what she will, until it is actually born into the world, so too will neither you nor I have any clear idea of what the other (with whom we have been pregnant all day) will look like or how the other will behave until that moment we meet again at the end of the day, in that daily birth or rebirth which is the encounter of the Husband and the Wife in the house and in the Marriage. And in this state of unending pregnancy so too must you take care not to eat things that will upset your stomach while at the same time keeping up your breathing exercises, resting when necessary, so that when the moment comes you will be in good physical condition, relaxed and fearless, and able to face the ordeal with the conviction that all will come out well. For to neglect these things in the daily pregnancy of the Marriage is to open oneself to the possibility of not only great pain but the premature or the miscarried as well, in which the image nurtured in pregnancy is too small or is ill formed in comparison with the strapping reality, suddenly strong and overpowering and demanding beyond all preconception.

22 ✄ Pots and Pans.

You are to keep
the pots and pans, and I mean by them the dishes and
all the cutlery such as the silverware or tableware as
well as cutting knives, skewers, and such widely diverse
items as mallets and pestles—anything, in short, you
must use in preparing food in the kitchen—all these
things you must keep in good order. It should be obvious
to you, as to anyone, how important it is to keep the pots
and pans clean inside and out, whether they be of aluminum, stainless steel, enamel, copper, cast iron, or any
combination of these elements, and well scoured so that
there is neither burnt food left on the inside nor stove
black on the outside; they are to be promptly washed
after each meal except in cases where the bottoms are
burnt, and they must be put to soak, and washed with
the appropriate solution of hot or cold water (hot is
generally the most effective) and soap or detergent, employing the abrasive action of washrag, plastic or metal
scouring pad or brush against the encrusted surfaces on
the inside and the blackened surfaces, if any, on the
outside; similarly for tableware, dishes of china, por-
celain, or varieties of common pottery, and miscellaneous
items of whatever materials they happen to be manu-
factured.

All this should be clear enough, and there is little more
I can add except to say that though I am aware of the
time consumed in washing up the pots and pans, it
would be well to remember that food, as it enters the
house as meat, poultry, dairy products, vegetable produce,
and so on, and as it eventually prances around the house
as combustion and growth, finally leaving the house as
garbage and excrement, is that without which the house

could not exist in any season or in any climate: as food of the house keeps the inhabitants from starving, so food of the Marriage keeps you and me from going hungry or starving, the Husband and the Wife.

And I, my dear, have taken upon myself as my duty to secure and bring in the food to the house from the garden where it grows (you may see the walls from your window) in the case of vegetables, or from the orchard in the case of fruits, or from the barnyard in the case of meat and dairy products, and to carry these things into the house and lay them down upon your sink board where you are to prepare them for cooking. Thus the preparation of the food can be said to begin when the seed is sown and not simply when the carrot, the cabbage, or the squash is laid upon your counter. Perhaps a better way to make this distinction would be to say that that part of the preparation of the food which takes place outdoors pertains to the male, that is, myself, while that part which takes place indoors pertains to you, the female —although it is indoors at the table in the kitchen that both of us sit down together and eat together the food that both of us have prepared, I at some distance in time and place, you more recently, a few minutes before, nearby, only a few feet away. Thus the food of Marriage —which in this respect resembles insemination and then much later the birth of the Children. Thus the food of Marriage.

23 ❧ The Refrigerator.

The refrigerator in the kitchen stands as an island of cold in a sea of warmth within its various skins of enamel, insulation, and plastic which serve to separate the two areas, the warm from the cool and freezing, the outside from the inside. Yet objects cannot be kept indefinitely in a refrigerator, generally reserved for the storing of fresh or relatively fresh food, because despite the cold within they will still spoil or lose their flavor or undergo unpleasant changes in shape, texture, or color. Thus the importance of arranging the food on the shelves and in the bins of the refrigerator in such a way that the older food is closest to the door and so will be taken out and prepared, eaten, served, or drunk before the newer or fresher food, which should be pushed to the back. In this way too, old food will not get shoved into the far corners of shelves or bins and become lost there until suddenly a stench begins leaking out of the box or until it is discovered when the refrigerator is defrosted, all shriveled up. This exercise should be performed every two weeks on the average in winter and every ten days in the summer and should be combined with a general cleaning out of the interior of the refrigerator, to include the washing of the trays and bins with hot soapy water and the enamel inside the box scrubbed with a solution of bicarbonate of soda and water. Throw out the old ice, refill the trays with fresh water—this is also advised, for old ice has a distinctive taste to the sensitive palate, having picked up the odors of various strong foods in the refrigerator despite their being wrapped up in several layers of foil or plastic—onions, cabbage, turnips, some cheeses, to mention a few—for there is virtually nothing that can stop a strong odor that is determined to move from place to place.

The refrigerator of the kitchen and thus of the house can be seen to represent the refrigerator of the Marriage, and by that I mean the repository of all such things as the Husband and the Wife wish to preserve against the effects of heat and time. You may wish to see it as a kind of memory or memory bank or joint account from which both of us may withdraw—or into which deposit—sustenance at any time. Indeed the vaultlike quality of the strong door with its gleaming nickel-plated latches and hinges can hardly suggest anything else, that this is the place where you and I keep what is dearest and of greatest value to the Marriage, that is, the joint memories. You must take care therefore not to deposit the sort of ill-wrapped food with strong odors that would infect the taste of the blander foods, and remember to clean out the interior at regular intervals in order to discourage the growth of fungi and molds. And as you open and close the door of the refrigerator and the light inside the box goes on and off, so too do you open and close the vault of our collective memory, that is, do you remember and forget, remember and forget. But it should not be left open for long periods of time, except when defrosting, so that its contents will not be unduly warmed up and thus spoil.

Nor should you crowd the refrigerator up with leftovers, needless to say, or foods that no one in the household will eat, or with foods that do not in fact need to be refrigerated at all—for the main function of refrigeration is to halt the growth and spread of microbes and bacteria of the sort that can make the eaters of the house sick or ill and in some cases even kill them, as in ptomaine and botulism. But in most foods there is no danger of this at all and they can simply be shelved in the cabinets or in the pantry, thus keeping the refrigerator from becoming overcrowded, not only in the kitchen but in the Marriage as well.

But we must not forget that food is grown from the earth in order to be eaten, and so what is put in the refrigerator is put there because it is intended to be taken out at some future date and be eaten up either cooked or raw. Cooking will take place either on the four burners of the stove or in its oven or both, which elements may be said to represent the inner life of the Wife, just as the garden may be said to represent the inner life of the Husband, that is, in those cases in which gardens are kept. Eating is what takes place at meals. One associates meals with placemats, silverware, dishes, and china, and the food that is served and eaten with these implements on a table by persons sitting in chairs and who now and then speak to each other between mouthfuls of food and drafts of water or wine. There are as many styles of eating as there are eaters, no doubt, but one of the most serviceable is to close the mouth once the food is inside it, whereupon you are to begin masticating or chewing in a relaxed manner, without haste. This throws the salivary glands into action. And once the food is ground into a pulp: swallow. If the food is well ground, the swallow will be smooth and effortless and you will hardly know what happened. Then you pause to have a sip of water or wine or whatever, after which it is wise to clear the throat discreetly so as to make room for the next swallow, that is, to clear away any loose ends. Of course this process of opening the mouth and taking in food and masticating it and swallowing it, to which may be added digestion and elimination, will be affected by the type of food to be so processed, whether tough and fibrous, crisp and brittle, soft and slippery, spicy or bland, and so on, all of which will also affect your speed. But that one should not eat with the mouth open and not speak with the mouth full are well-known principles universally accepted, and I need add nothing to them except to say that beneath them lie even yet greater truths. For the food that is cooked and served at meals can be seen to represent the food of the Marriage, by which I mean the language of the Marriage, and so it is no wonder that the greater part of the eating and the talking takes place at the same time, at meals, with the Husband speaking across the table while his mouth is empty and the Wife listening while hers is full, then speaking when hers is empty and the Husband's full—in short, the manner in which I have often recommended that we converse at our three meals taken together, breakfast, lunch, and dinner.

For if food at the table represents the language of the Marriage with the various courses representing the parts of speech, with prepositions and articles and conjunctions built around the main course of verbs and nouns, many of which have just come from the refrigerator of the Marriage, and the whole meal composing a sentence or a statement that begins with an apéritif (the capital letter) and ends with a period (cup of coffee), then it should be clear how important it is to prepare and utter your words well and to know when to open your mouth and when to close it—when to speak and when not to speak. You should no more blurt out an ill-formed sentence, for example, than you should throw together a dinner in five minutes out of leftovers and stale food to serve up to an honored guest: good sentences, like good meals, require that their ingredients be kept well stored and be prepared with great care and consideration, with delicate sauces and dressings, but not overly seasoned, and be served on attractive plates whose rims are wiped clean of dribbled gravy, but with confidence and without apology. But is your guest a vegetarian? Is he on a diet today, not taking sugar or salt? Do tomatoes give him hives? Bananas nausea? Does ice cream make his hands and feet swell up? Better to know these things in advance than to find you have poisoned your guest who out of politeness has eaten everything you have served up and who now grows more and more silent as his sufferings increase, to a point finally where he is unable to say anything at all.

24 ❧ Leftovers.

Dinner plates, salad plates, forks, spoons, knives, salt and pepper shakers—and then there is a whole vast area of drinking vessels, water glasses, wine glasses, tea cups, coffee mugs—all things which you must remove from the table as soon as they have been finished with, carrying them to the sink board, where they must be scraped clean and immersed in water hot to the touch and agitated and abraded insofar as is necessary to remove coatings or particles of food, then rinsed in clear cold or hot water, placed in a rack to drain, wiped dry-to-the-touch with small towels you are to provide especially for the purpose, put away in their cupboards, racks, or hung from hooks in some cases, such things you learn to do automatically in time, without complaint, day after day, whether you are there alone or whether I am at your side encouraging you, suggesting ways in which you might carry out such tasks more quickly and more efficiently. There should be no leftovers in principle, or if there are I do not wish to know of them, just as I must judge expertly in advance the quantities of food you will need from the garden, for example, and not bring in and lay upon the sink counter quantities of lettuce or carrots or squash that might clog the refrigerator for a week, growing limp and rubbery and thus inedible—only to end up in the garbage pail, with the leftovers, which is to be carried down to the geese and the contents dumped out over the fence to them. For it would be well to see the geese in their pen as being the geese of the Marriage, that is, all those who stand to benefit from the scraps and leftovers of discord or disunion and grow fat upon them, with their cackling of mockery and rejoicing. Therefore if you and I be in a state of harmony, you preparing what I harvest with exactitude, and I eating what you have prepared in just the right amount, then the geese of Marriage will be lean and silent.

In general the taste of the food should be more pleasing to my palate than to yours, since you, being in the kitchen all day, may eat whatever you like at any time, unlike myself, who must toil distantly in the fields, as it were. Similarly when I am satisfied in the palate and you too are satisfied in the palate, then together we are better able to judge the quality of the food of other Marriages by this simple rule, that if the food tastes bad, then the Marriage in question is good, while if the food tastes good, then the Marriage in question is bad—what I have come to call "second and third helping Marriages."

25 🥀 Weeds. I have taken it upon myself, as you know, to grow our food in the garden that lies between the house and the river (the garden whose walls you can see from your window), in the rich alluvial soil deposited there millennia ago. There, where the high walls shield me from passersby and other distractions, I have been able to plant, fertilize, irrigate, cultivate, and harvest, to assure that what is planted sprouts, what sprouts grows, what grows yields, and what yields is brought up into the kitchen and presented to you, and to guard against pests, predators, and intruders of all sorts. To these ends I have chosen to cultivate not only the walled garden but the rest of the yard as well, with such implements as I deem necessary to maintain the tilth of the soil and prevent the growth of weeds, and these implements are not only my two hands themselves but those generally known as "hand" implements, usually consisting of a wooden handle, often ashwood, with a metal fixture at one or both ends and with which the earth is cut, sliced, abraded, tamped, stroked, poked, pushed and pulled, flung, and rolled over, in addition to implements known as "power" implements such as tractors and tillers which generally churn the earth, and whose motors you easily hear anywhere in the house as an explosive *putt-putt* sound. It has been said that no plant is a weed everywhere and that every plant is a weed somewhere, but the generally recognized characteristics of weeds are their ability to strangle "plants" and crowd them out with the result that the size of the yield and the quality of the fruit are likely to be reduced, and this is why weeds are undesirable. Weeds of the garden and yard spring from seeds that have been brought in from outside as borne on currents of air

or by flows of water, such as down the irrigation ditches or by other means—adhering to the soles of shoes and to the undersides of cars and trucks and passing domestic animals as well as wild ones, and dropped there, about the yard, in a casual and usually unintentional manner. And there in the soil through the natural processes that involve the moving of the soil (freezing, thawing) and the dampening and drying out of it, there the seeds of weeds will sprout and send down roots, send up shoots, and eventually take over the whole yard if they are not first cultivated under—and choke out the various ornamental plants and shrubs of the yard and the vegetables of the garden and fill both with painful thorns, stickers, thistles, and barbs, which become a considerable fire hazard in the dry winds of autumn.

As with both the garden behind its cinder-block walls and the yard which surrounds the house, so too with the Marriage: I have taken it upon myself as Husband to cultivate our Marriage and keep it free of weeds, not only to increase the yield of succulent vegetables and vegetation pleasing to look at but to reduce the potential for fire as well. But since I cannot stop the passage of stray animals across the yard except by putting up fences of fine mesh all around the property or except by extending the vegetable garden walls to enclose the whole property, both at exorbitant cost—for even a field mouse can bear a seed of a weed tucked into its fur—nor can I easily lock the gate against all visitors who might bear seeds dragging from the undersides of their cars, for it would bar too those who came in clean cars, with clean soles; so in the same way, as Husband and male, must I bear with the random traffic of comers and goers up the drive and through the yard, some of whom harbor seeds and others of whom do not, for though the putting up of tight fences and high walls and locked gates might eventually result in our Marriage being free of "weeds," there will always be that unending reservoir of seeds hidden away in the very soil itself, some of which have lain there dormant for hundreds of years and where they will always lie patiently awaiting the moment when you and I will think our yard is at last free of weeds and then, and only then, will sprout.

26 🍃 Fences.

Yet this is no reason to neglect the barbed-wire fences that surround the property, for I am well aware of the importance of keeping them in good repair by regularly noting the condition of the fence-posts, whether rotting or not, where the staples are coming loose or have fallen out, where wires have broken, and so on. A fence whose posts are rotting at the bottom cannot be expected to stand for long against the high winds of spring without falling down, and likewise a fence whose strands of barbed wire are weak and rusty is likely to give way whenever the stray cow or horse pushes its head through the fence to munch on the succulent grasses growing within, thus admitting the whole herd and devastating the garden—or be gradually pulled to the ground by the yearly growth of creeper and wild grape. Thus, deeply dug holes, sound posts, good wire, tight staples may be said to compose the essential ingredients of the good fence that is well maintained, in addition to a solid gate, that is, one that swings open and closes easily, latches securely, locks irrevocably.

So too with the fences that surround or enclose the Marriage, which may be called the fences of Marriage, whose function is not to exclude or prevent the friend from coming into and going out of the property so much as to screen out his dogs, goats, sheep, cattle, horses, and whatever else might be inclined to follow upon his heels. For you will find it easy enough to imagine that the friend who travels around and pays visits with all his animals can do nothing but bring down misfortune on the heads of those he visits, for they will find their trees stripped of bark, their ornamentals trampled, their fields ravaged, haystacks knocked over, septic tanks caved in, wells fouled. Thus the fences of Marriage may be seen to be a kind of filter through which certain large animals are unable to pass.

Therefore when our friends come to call—rare enough as this is—it is best that you or I ask them to leave their herds down on the road and to make sure they close the gate securely on their way in, even if they intend to take only a minute or two paying their respects. Likewise I will not encourage them to overstay their visits to the point of causing their herds to become restless or exasperated, in which state they can easily charge or butt down the gate and fan out over the yard. A half an hour in summer and an hour in winter is a good rule, supposing the weather to be clear or dry. In bad weather these times may be easily doubled without fear of undue stress upon the fences of the Marriage against which the Husband and the Wife lean to one side, the friend leaning from the other, that is, from opposite directions. For fences, like all such things, are best not put to extreme tests too often —no more than a person should rush out bright and early every morning and tug at the wires of his fence with his tractor, by means of a cable or chain, to make sure they are still as strong as they were the day before. Sooner or later they will snap under such treatment, and the fence will then be in need of major repairs, a tedious business calling for heavy leather gloves to protect the hands from the wire barbs, and crowbars, pliers, fence pullers, new posts, new wire, new staples.

27 🐾 The Vegetable Garden. I

have asked you not to venture into the vegetable garden unescorted, for there is no way I could possibly instruct you in advance, at a distance, where and where not to step at any given time. Its plan is not only intricate but fluctuates according to the seasons as well, with certain patches and rows being planted in the spring but not in the summer but yet again in the autumn, and others being planted only in summer and yet others only in winter, all along revolving lines that are, at times, complex beyond even my immediate grasp. Thus, supposing you had free access and free rein, should I one day say to you, "You may step there," all would no doubt go well and you would step there as instructed that particular day and not elsewhere, but then the following day everything could be entirely different and you, still thinking it was safe to step "there," would proceed to step "there"—only to discover, as I would point out, you had crushed underfoot some seedling I had transplanted in the cool of the previous evening. And not only that, for what may seem to be a path, being graveled, raised, and bordered, may not be in fact a path at all—may be an experimental strip of rock mulch—though might too be a graveled path—while what may not seem a path, some band of grassy growth, may in fact be a path after all—or not—in the form of a strip of cover cropping that is serving temporarily (or not) as a path or other passageway. Similarly you are not likely to know what vegetables are to be picked and what not picked, and where they should be thinned or where cleaned out completely to prepare for a successive planting, and so on, without the sort of detailed indications whose daily preparation in writing would take far more of my time than I could spare, for the complexity of the garden is such —however small it may seem to you in the brief moments you spend there in my company—that there is no other way the situation could possibly be covered. To pick a lettuce? But which row? Which lettuce? The large or the small? Where to step on the way to the row, to the specific lettuce? At what hour? And so on with carrots, beets, squash, corn, tomatoes, and peppers, the picking of which, if done randomly, without plan or schedule and in ignorance of the true state of the garden, would result in a subtle devastation of all that grows there within a very short period of time. Thus not only have I requested that you not enter the garden casually as if walking into a store where you might take certain items off the shelves to put into your basket, but also that you not touch or pick the vegetables except in those cases now and then when I may indicate exactly which squash or bean should be picked, which carrot pulled, which lettuce or cabbage cut at the root, and how they should be picked, pulled, or cut, whereupon you certainly should feel free to proceed to do so if you wish.

28 ❧ The Goats.

The animals of the barn-yard, particularly the goats, may be said to represent the animals or herds of the Marriage but in a way which is perhaps not normal in our Marriage, given the fact that most people keep only cats and dogs. But in our case the goats are the true animals of the barnyard, thus of the Marriage, because of their substantial contribution to the household and the garden as well as the amount of care they require in order to yield at full capacity. And as it is with the goats of the barnyard, so it is with those of the Marriage, by which I mean the genitalia, which the Husband and the Wife must keep confined or penned up most of the time while also taking care to feed them well with daily rations of fodder of the appropriate kind so that they yield up and produce the protein-rich products which they manufacture out of mere grasses and dried leaves—milk and manure. Their care is daily and exacting, for it involves leading them out of their pen twice a day one by one, in an order which they understand, to be fed their grain on the milkstand. Here those that have been fresh-ened, those whose bags are swollen and tight, must be milked, while those who are pregnant and expectant, with bags small and wrinkled, should of course not be milked—but all must be promptly led back into the pen, and the gate locked with both the latch and the chain. Then there is the frequent trimming of their hooves and the clipping of hair around the udders, as well as the cleaning out of the pens in the springtime and the carting of the manure into the walled garden to be scattered across the earth and plowed under. Negligence can take two forms, and you will observe this as being more common and widespread than you would be inclined to believe, but if you look carefully you will see the signs everywhere. The first case is failing to feed the animals and failing to give them water at regular intervals, which can be compounded by failing to clean out their pens or to treat them for the various maladies they are subject to, such as worms and scours. In this case the animals wither and die. In the second case, where the pens are not kept in good repair, the wire netting allowed to rip and tear, the boards to loosen and break, the goats will be seen breaking out of the pen and making straight for the grain barrels. There they will gorge themselves to the point of bloating, and also die. Or else they will rush headlong through the barbed-wire fence and tear their udders, with similar results. Thus the animals of the barnyard, like those of the Marriage, must remain in confinement except at such regularly scheduled times when they are led out of their pens to be milked or groomed or fed, and put back into their pens when such tasks are complete, and not allowed to roam freely about the yard. And as you and I have our goats, so will other Marriages have their cattle or rabbits or pigeons or doves, or even bees. Nonetheless, despite apparent differences, the principles remain essentially the same.

29 ✺ Tools.

As you are the sole or at least principal mistress over the vessels, implements, and tools of the kitchen and need not listen to any other advice except my own concerning their use and care, and this includes brooms (I believe there are two), dustpans, the vacuum cleaner, dust mops, and toilet brushes, so I have taken it upon myself to be the master of the tools to be found elsewhere on the property, including garden tools and implements, general repair and maintenance tools including automotive, none of which is to be loaned out in my absence without my express written or verbal permission in which I designate not only the name of the borrower and the name of the tool but the time during which it may be borrowed as well, all of which information it is my custom to enter into a clothbound book for future reference.

The importance of tools should not be underestimated, for without them I cannot plow the garden or cultivate it, and the house and outbuildings and garden walls and fences themselves cannot be repaired or expanded with new construction or additions or even dismantled when found to be derelict, obsolete, or in the way; and so it is with good reason that I regard the loss of a tool as a tragedy of the first magnitude. It would be well for you to make note therefore of the ways in which tools can be lost, such as by accidental and unseen dropping into growths of weeds, or by being left in a high (or low) and thus normally unseen place from the point of view of eye level, or by being moved from one place to another by a person or agency other than the current user of the tool—who then returns to find the tool gone—or by pure and simple theft, to name a few. Although these conditions perhaps more generally apply to outside tools than to inside ones, you will detect enough similarities to find them useful. And recovery in these cases will be a matter of patient searching or of finding which occurs when weeds die back, snow melts, rivers recede, or the light of day follows upon the dark of night.

I regard, you should know, my tools as an extension of my hand, that is, as sentient organs (the expression "to lend a hand" comes to mind), so that it is necessary for me to ascertain in advance whether my tools will or will not be abused in some way such as by being pounded upon, squeezed harshly, heated up, rubbed or cooled down in such a way as to cause "pain" or injury to the tool; and I see the ideal borrower, who can perhaps never exist, as being one who will handle my tools in such a way as to cause them "pleasure" by taking care of them in the prescribed manner, that is, by polishing them, sharpening them, keeping them warm or cool, supplying them with the proper nutrients (gasoline, water) and lubricants (oil, grease) when and where needed, so that they are returned in a condition of gleaming radiance.

It follows then that you should not fall into the habit of borrowing kitchen tools or implements or vessels from any of the neighbors, no more than I the other kind, and I will say the same of the supplies to be brought in from town, for the ideal Marriage is one in which nothing is either lent to outsiders or borrowed from them. For as the tools of the household, so the tools of the Marriage, which if not used properly can have their blades dulled, their points blunted through loss of edge or loss of temper, air chambers punctured, and so on—for the tools of the Marriage, if kept in good order, serve to keep weeds from the garden of Marriage and to keep the vehicles of Marriage in good running order and the house of Marriage in good repair, dry and without leaks, and so on, and thus requiring no borrowing of others on any account.

30 🦢 Visits.

Nonetheless politeness or common courtesy dictates that you and I together must now and then pay a call in order to demonstrate that we are human beings—weak and lonely—like any other, and it might be well to consider how to deport yourself on one of these rare occasions when we display the Marriage to the public eye. It is of course impossible to take with us on these visits the house itself, that is, the place where we are most accustomed to stand united with all appearances well maintained, the furniture in place, the windowsills dusted, and the bric-a-brac polished and ready for admiration. Yet one can go on a visit bearing a gift and preferably something carefully chosen to be an object that will not only prove useful and attractive to our hosts but will indicate as well the joy, the abundance, the unity of our own Marriage—bushels of squash, baskets of lettuce, bunches of onions or garlic, cheeses, cakes, and pies all come to mind here, and ideally perhaps a hamper made up of selections from each. It would be wise of you also to take along some mending to work on while you talk, and you may also choose to bring along the bread dough to rise in the back seat of the car—this will be bound to make a good impression—which you will now and then go out to, in order to punch down. In this connection, you might find it useful to bring along a mechanical timer with a bell. But should there be no mending to be done or bread to be risen, surely there will be shoes or silverware to be polished, or potatoes peeled, or a small quantity of handwashing to be done, or any number of little tasks that are easily portable, for it is important as the Marriage moves out of the house which is its own and drives down the road and enters into the house of another Marriage that it retain as many of the appearances outside the house as it is accustomed to maintaining within—rather than fling everything to the winds. And thus too the little tokens of affection exchanged in the Marriage house should neither be abandoned while abroad in other Marriages, so to speak, and should I indicate in one way or another that I am ready for my coffee or lunch or dinner, the hour having struck, it will not be out of place for you to suggest to the hostess that she step aside a moment while you prepare me my coffee or lunch or dinner from the ingredients you might make a note of carrying along in a small basket or box. As you know well, I eat rapidly and the whole meal will vanish in a flash and be scarcely noticed by our hosts, and it will take you no time at all to wash the dishes quickly in their sink and dry them with their towel. Our afternoon naps can similarly be taken in such a way as not to disrupt the other Marriage, myself first, you second, so that while one naps the other can carry on the conversation in a low voice.

Thus these visits, if well prepared for in advance, can serve to strengthen the Marriage rather than weaken it or dilute it by filling it with strange objects and sensations, for the value in packing the car with various gifts and possessions and supplies to take along is that they provide familiar matter out of which to make conversation with the Marriage being visited, that is, the Children, the laundry, the mending, the shoes, the fruits and vegetables of the Marriage, things about which you will find yourself able to converse with great ease and fluency, thus creating a solid impression of the Marriage as one which can undergo a wide variety of circumstances and changes without suffering any ill effects at all.

Second

*To My Son Concerning
the Conduct of His
Childhood*

1 🦋 Disturbances.

You know how little I like to be disturbed at anything I may be doing, but there are certain times you may disturb me without my minding, among which is after dinner as I lie upon the couch digesting. Thus reclining, I am most able to see the room and all its furnishings at the level of your own eyes; also I find it easier to listen to the grunts and gurglings and other noises on the way to being words I myself once used to make, I suppose.

2 ❧ Putting Toys Away.

You are to make an effort to put away your toys after each use, that is, back into the boxes and onto the shelves whence they came, so that I or other members of the household will not trip or stumble over them or be forced to make long detours across your room or wherever else you may have left them. Toys are to be played with (imagine what is small and insignificant to be large and powerful, for example) and not to be employed as implements or weapons or anything else; thus a toy left carelessly about, blocking a hallway or threshold, is likely to seem something else, that is, an irritation or an obstacle or a barrier.

3 🎀 Taking Toys Out.

Although it may seem more rewarding to take your toys down off their shelves or out of your toy box or toy closet and spread them around the room than it will to gather them up and put them back into their proper places, small toys on the shelves, medium-size toys in the box, large toys in the closet, the latter task is in fact more rewarding because it lends itself to the prospect—the anticipation—the hope—of the former, as in being able to say to oneself once again: "Now or at any time in the near future I may take my toys out and spread them around the room," a thing you cannot say to yourself when your toys are in fact actually spread out across the floor and in which state they are forever droning away at you: "Soon you must put us back into our proper places." Thus in making the pleasant task the unpleasant to a degree and the unpleasant the pleasant, a small and minor—but nonetheless important—victory.

4 ✿ Storing Toys.

You should see the various shelves and boxes and trunks, and even the closet, of your room as being the various boxes, shelves, and closets of your Childhood, that is, those places in which you accumulate and keep stored pleasant and agreeable memories for later times of need when you are older and grown up, at a time when you will find it less easy to acquire pleasant memories, let alone store them up. Thus, to keep your toys put away in their proper places so that they will not be accidentally stepped on, tripped over, or thrown out is also to keep the things you will remember in the future put away in a safe place until such times as you may really need to take them out and use them and when it will be important that they are in as good a condition as possible, free from the ravages of time and neglect.

By the same token you should not let your various toy storage areas become clogged with whatever ephemeral debris you may happen to pick up on your wanderings about the house or the yard, such as pebbles, feathers, bits of wood, dead insects, leaves, and so on—in short, all things which you may see as being of utmost fascination now but which later, as you grow older, will come to seem of no interest at all. The accumulation of pleasant memories is hard work and requires great discipline, not to speak of a discriminating eye, and you would do well to see your Childhood as a time when you are selecting and wrapping up and putting aside those things which later, as an adult, you will wish to take down from the shelves and out of the closet and unwrap and display, as a sort of gift to yourself across the years. The good Childhood will therefore be one in which the memory is well chosen for its design and durability, the excellence of its materials, while the bad Childhood will on the contrary lay up only those things which, over the years, will seem no more than what they have always been, the little shells, the husks, the dry carcasses cast aside by the flood of life.

5 🦢 The Room. It has been said that Childhood is a room in the House of Marriage or the house of the family, and so you may wish to see your room in the house, which is next to your Sister's room, as being in fact the room of your Childhood, that is, the place where the greater part of your Childhood will take place. I cannot easily overemphasize the importance of this time in your life, and this is why I (and your Mother) have set aside a room especially for this purpose, even before the age at which you may become aware of the fact that this room, with its door and window, its floor and ceiling, its four walls, closet, and light fixture, is your room and no one else's and will always be yours—although your progress with the word "mine" seems to be going well. Yet in bestowing this room upon you, the room which is your Childhood, I am also bestowing upon you certain obligations that naturally go along with the room, as they would with any room to be used for any purpose similarly bestowed, and that is to keep it clean and tidy at all times, neat and in good repair. For a room in which toys have been scattered all over the floor, whose walls have been scribbled up, and whose ceiling is spattered with paint and otherwise marked by the impact of various objects, is a Childhood in which walls, ceiling, and floor have also been defaced and littered, that is, a Childhood in which (because of the mess) no one will wish to stay for very long.

Thus to keep a clean room is to keep a clean Childhood, or one within which you will be contented to stay for as long as you wish and in and out of which others, such as your Mother and myself, will pass freely and pleasantly and even linger for longer or shorter periods of time, sit down on the end of your little bed or on one of your toy trunks, to admire the neatness and tidiness of the room.

6 ❧ Large and Small Toys.

You should also make an effort to see your toys, which are both the toys of your room and the toys of your Childhood, as representatives of the larger objects which you will have to manipulate later in life, so that in manipulating them now, in reduced scale, you can slowly build up the experience necessary to manipulate them later in your life, in true scale. You will notice, for example, how your toys increase gradually in size through the years until at last they will be full scale, all going well. You will also see this process taking place in your friends as they grow from the small to the large, as well as in yourself, now small but eventually to be full size. And similarly as the goal of real life is to amass whatever number and kind of objects are necessary for your well-being, so too the goal of Childhood is to amass sufficient toys, that is, representatives of those objects you will strive to obtain in reality. Thus it is of utmost importance to fix your desires upon the right toy, in the right order, and this is why I have set aside a certain time at the very end of each day to go over the mail-order catalogs with you, pointing to the pictures of what I suggest you should desire, reading out the descriptions to you, quoting the prices.

7 🌿 Trash.

I particularly request in advance that you do not hang around trash barrels, whether they be those at the end of the drive or next door, or the little "dumps" to be found up and down the dirt road, that is, when you will be of the age to wander that far. Not only can you cut your hands and feet on the various broken bottles or sharp edges of tin cans and other refuse, with the virtual certainty of infection, you are also likely to track the gummy residues of such places right into the house, either on your shoes or on your cuffs, or both, and thus endanger the health of everyone. The small metallic object embedded in the pavement or found at the edge of the road or down at the river, so long as it is clear it has been well cleansed by the action of the sun or water—I have no objection to your bringing back to the house and even into your room. You may wish to become an archaeologist or a mining engineer, and this is as good a place to begin as any. But in the meantime, stay away from trash. The distinction between what is trash and what is good is, I admit, a difficult one. But it is not impossible. Perhaps you should look upon trash as that which someone does not want or no longer desires. It follows then that you should not desire it either. What is good and therefore not trash is what everyone desires but yet not everyone can have and, as a result, is not to be found in trash barrels.

8 ❦ Progress.

As the toys of your Childhood, in the shape of cars and trucks and ships and airplanes, rockets, helicopters, trains, barnyards, and so on, represent these objects in full scale as you will come to them later in life, it follows that as you take care of your toys now so you will later take care of the things of reality, that is, by putting them away when not in use and by not taking a rock to them to see what is inside (usually nothing, as you will find out) or not leaving them out in the rain or snow to rust or otherwise decay. The bowl of nuts on the kitchen table is there for a specific purpose, and whenever the urge comes over you to pry open one of your toys or to disembowel it, the best thing to do is to go to the kitchen table and crack a few nuts until the urge passes, as inevitably it will.

However, as the objects and things you desire are not merely objects and things, being rather ideas that have been precipitated out of time and space into matter in much the same way nitrogen is precipitated out of the atmosphere and rained down on the garden by thunder and lightning, that is by electrical discharges in the sky, if you follow me, so too must you look at the objects and things that come your way *not* as absolute and perfect and finished so much as stages in a process leading to perfection, that is, in a progressive series of which each succeeding member is gradually less imperfect in the way that the toy airplane made out of plastic is an imperfect version of the model airplane without a motor, and in turn an imperfect version of one with a motor, and in turn an imperfect version (given several removes) of a small real airplane, and so on up the series, to the jet airliner of reality you will eventually pilot in reality, supposing your desires lead you to become a jet airline pilot, supposing there be jets, airlines, pilots, air, world—at that time—but just supposing. Thus to pass from the one to the other in the series is a sign of progress, and I attach no stigma to whatever desires you may have to destroy earlier and more primitive objects in the series because you regard them as old-fashioned and obsolete in relation to your then-current stage of raised consciousness.

9 🐍 The Wagon.

You have begun, I believe, to pull your wagon around the yard and so have learned or will shortly learn the value of keeping its little wheels on the various garden paths and on the driveway, rather than letting them stray into ditches or become hooked on posts and tree trunks, from which it is often difficult to extricate them. By keeping to the path you will also experience the pleasant sensation of wheels rolling over smooth surfaces, both by towing the wagon behind you or by sitting in it and being pushed or by rolling down a slight incline on your own. But the main thing at the beginning is not to go too fast; otherwise you are likely to tip over and run into a rock or other object that might damage your wagon, or injure your feet by trying to drag yourself to a stop when you are going too fast to do so. The best way to propel yourself in your wagon, you will find—for there is not always someone around who will push you up and down the paths, and you will not always feel like climbing up a hill and coasting down it—is to kneel with one leg in the wagon, with one hand grasping the rim of the wagon body, and then push with the foot on the ground. This will not work, however, where the ground is sandy or wet or muddy, nor are you advised to make sharp left-hand turns (supposing you are right-handed) in this position under any conditions except when traveling very slowly. Once you have mastered this position, you can easily spend the greater part of the day propelling yourself about the yard, most of whose paths I have paved in cement exactly for this purpose.

And you will do well to watch me as I oil the wagon's wheels and tighten its screws and nuts every now and then so that you yourself can soon do these simple maintenance tasks, without which the wheels will squeak and turn stiffly, nuts and screws fall off and be lost in the grass, and eventually cause the handle or axles to drop off at a time when you may most need them. But more important, I will know by such signs that you are ready to move up to your tricycle, a machine more complex and delicate than your wagon but one which is at the same time more self-propelled than the other, more comfortable, and smoother riding. Yet it is also more dangerous, and you must learn that sharp turns in either direction are to be avoided, and that regular maintenance is even more critical. And it, like your wagon before it, you should make an effort to keep on the back porch in that parking place I have already reserved for it, beneath the wooden plaque that bears your name, those hours when you are not actually riding it, so that it will not suffer unnecessarily from the effects of the sun or rain.

10 🐝 Bicycles.

Next, the bicycle. You will have three of these—a one-speed, a three-speed, and a ten-speed—evenly spaced out over your bicycle-riding days, which will be upon you before you know it. These, like all your toys, clothes, shoes, and so on, your Mother and I have already purchased in advance—they are stored in the cinder-block shed in the backyard and are arranged in trunks and boxes in chronological order, up to age fifteen —so that should the financial status of the family be threatened at any time or should any critical items become unavailable because of national or international shortages, you will not have your Childhood supplies cut off. The care of your bicycle will be even more demanding, since there are tires fat and thin to keep properly inflated, brakes and gears adjusted, chains and sprockets and bearings oiled, and seats and handlebars raised or lowered. However, you will have received some experience in these matters with your tricycle, and it will be a simple matter to adjust your knowledge upwards, as it were, to the bicycle. And I will be at hand explaining the way in which to loosen and tighten nuts and bolts and how to avoid cross-threading them, how to check tire pressures, inspect the treads, check the tension of the various cables and chains, and so on, and within a short time you will be able to carry out these tasks, which can easily take up half a riding day, providing you wish to keep your machine or machines in good order.

And as the wagon is but preparation for the tricycle, and the tricycle for the bicycle or bicycles, so is the bicycle preparation of a sort for the automobile, the machine in which you will launch yourself out into the world at large, down the path of life. But as you have been practicing its

use from a very early age, by the time you slip behind
the wheel of your own car you will know instinctively what
to do and will probably need little other instruction—for
by then all those long hours spent pushing toy cars back
and forth on the rug and the arms of chairs and on table-
tops and along the roads of your sandpile will have added
up, drawn interest and matured, and so on—and the maintenance practices you will have learned with your wagons,
tricycle, and bicycles will be easily applicable to your automobile or at least to many parts and functions of it. The
main difference is that your automobile will be provided
with a motor whose care and feeding you should not take
lightly, as I will explain at the proper time. The internal
combustion engine is a delicate and often troublesome
mechanism, and it would be unwise of me to allow you to
set off down the path of life without first drawing you
aside and explaining to you all the things that can go
wrong with pistons, cylinders, bearings, valves, crank-
shafts, carburetors, generators, starters, and so on. The list
of their ailments is interminable, and you would do well in
the meanwhile to spend as much time as you can peering
under the hood of the family car during those days I am
repairing or servicing the motor, in order at least to begin
learning the names of the moving parts—that is, as soon
as you are tall or strong enough to be able to stand on the
bumper or on a box to watch for extended periods of time.

11 🍃 Many and Few Toys.

In the course of your Childhood you will notice that some of your friends will have not good toys and that others will be outfitted with the best that money can buy, and there may be others among your acquaintances who have virtually nothing and so must amuse themselves with sticks and little pebbles and dry flowers. In any case, there will always be those who have toys worse and better than your own. And here, a useful lesson to life. For those rich in toys today may not become rich in goods later on unless they put their minds to it, and thus they can be easily overtaken by those poor in toys today who are truly determined to become released from their present bondage as children, toyless or nearly so; and so if you see the toy as the seed planted in the ground which will sprout and grow into a luxuriant shape later on if well watered and manured, then it is clear that the poor seed can produce the abundant plant, if well watered and manured, while the rich seed can equally produce the weak and spindly plant, if poorly watered and manured. Thus there is always hope. Do not envy your friend next door who may be richer now in toys than you. He may in time become bored with his own desires too easily satisfied, while yours may remain keen and fresh—and eventually you will remember him only as the boy who had good toys.

Desires, you will learn also, must be carefully pruned like anything else, for without pruning, the first growth may be fast and spectacular while the later growth becomes a self-defeating tangle of leaves and branches vainly thrashing for light and air—while the well-pruned tree with its branches amply spaced so as to allow the free passage of sunlight and air, though a slower starter, will end up putting out a heavier set of blossoms and bearing more and better fruit than the other. This is also true as regards fertilizer. That is, the young tree too heavily fertilized is likely to put on excessive growth during the summer months, thus overextending itself and exposing itself to being disastrously frozen back in the winter. And so also with toys, when there are too many.

12 🐝 **The Garden.** The cultivation of desires in the garden of life, like that of vegetables, is continuous and unending work. From time to time you drag your wagon down the path to the walled garden and look through the cracks in the wooden gate to see if I am working in there, and then drag your wagon back up to the house. So no doubt you have an idea. And work may be seen as play frozen into routine, that is, what takes place at certain fixed hours at a fixed place and for which one receives a reward that is certain as compared to one that is uncertain—or often, oddly enough, no reward at all. But in the case of the garden the reward is the various vegetables that are yielded up, such as lettuce, carrots, squash, cabbage, corn, and tomatoes, to name a few, in exchange for the labor performed there, the labor of planting, cultivating, fertilizing, and harvesting—an arrangement that is eminently fair and just and exactly as it should be. For no more would I wish to labor in a garden, hoeing and cultivating and fertilizing, in which nothing at all had been planted and from which therefore nothing could be harvested, than I would wish to drink from a glass without water or eat from a bowl without soup, to refer to situations with which you might be a little more familiar. But in the garden, as in the garden of life, there will be certain creatures who will seek to cheat and swindle you out of your harvest and yield, and I mean by them the pests, garden pests, namely aphids, squash bugs, cucumber beetles, bean beetles, cutworms, corn earworms, tomato worms, who will eat up the leaves of the plant or suck them dry or eat the vegetables themselves—or any or all combinations of those—thus causing a drop in water pressure in the stems and foliage (known as "wilting")

or the rotting of the vegetables on the vine or the general defoliation of the plant. So too in the garden of life will you find your desires, which are represented by the plants, attacked by varieties of sucking, nibbling, or chewing pests who will seek to cheat or swindle you out of the fruits of the harvest and against whom there is no protection except to keep your garden clean and its refuse well composted, to speak organically, and thus the plants healthy to begin with, for the pest attacking the healthy plant is much less likely to do harm.

But perhaps I do not make myself clear. In the garden of life the plants represent the desires which, when cultivated conscientiously for a set period of time, flower and fruit. The pests then are all those who would hinder and thwart this process, causing the desires to wilt, grow weak and die, thus not flower, not fruit.

13 🦋 **Walls.** It is to keep out the larger predators—notably rabbits—that there is a high cinder-block wall around the vegetable garden, a wall that serves equally to exclude the casual visitor who would be tempted to wander up and down the rows admiring the vegetables while completely unaware that he or she might be trampling down some just-emerging seedlings. And as you know, I keep the wooden gate locked at all times, from inside or out, depending on whether I am inside the garden or outside, and you are requested not even to attempt to enter the garden except in the company of your Mother, who has been instructed not to enter the garden except at my invitation and in my presence. Gardening requires patience and discipline and the manipulation of complex tools and equipment and the keeping of exact records, and these qualities and practices are best developed in solitude, not in the presence of others too easily prone to chatter and question. For you have no doubt seen through the cracks that I do not garden lightly and unarmed, though I imagine it will be some time before you understand the reasons for my complex movements or even understand how complex they are in the first place. The loose-fitting light-colored garden clothing I keep in the shed inside the walls, the broad leather belt from which hang my trowel and weed hook and pruning knife and first-aid kit, the pouch containing pens, pencils, and my notebook for jotting down garden notes, the bundle of white plastic markers upon which I scribble brief reminders to myself and which I thrust into the earth at the various trouble spots as they come up, and even the small pellet pistol that I use to discourage the grosbeaks that strip the pods of their peas and peck holes in the fruit

of the dwarf trees espaliered against the white walls—
all these tools and implements and devices I may use
within an hour or so on a particularly busy summer day, to
name just the few of them I always carry about on my person and not to speak of those I keep in the toolshed, the
hoes, the shovels, the rakes, the pitchforks, the seeders, the
tillers, the dusters, and the shredder.

For the garden must not only be planted and harvested,
it must also be weeded and thinned and irrigated and composted and manured at various times throughout the year;
otherwise the plants will not grow well, or will not grow
at all. And so too with the garden of desires which, like
the garden of reality, should be walled up as high as is
necessary to keep you from being distracted by passersby,
who will without fail—should your garden be without
walls—stand on the edge and admire your vegetables, the
size of your squash or onions, the rich green of your lettuce
and spinach, the height of your corn, to the point that you
may have to interrupt your work in order to ply them with
gifts of your produce—or who will delight in offering you
advice on how to increase your yields or eliminate certain
pests or how to grow crops you have absolutely no wish to
grow—until finally they render your own garden unrecognizable to yourself, either because nothing grows there
anymore that you wish to taste or to eat or because you
have been induced to give it all away, leaving nothing at
all for yourself.

14 ❦ Preservation.

By the same token, what is gotten out of the garden of life must be kept and preserved exactly as the produce of the garden—the garden—the garden-garden—is preserved, that is, by canning, freezing, drying or dehydrating, and by storage in root cellars or in other places suitable to the characteristics of the food to be preserved as well as the length of time it is to be preserved. There is no trick, for example, in preserving an apple for one day or even two or three. The trick comes in hanging on. For there will be periods of time when the garden of life is dormant and not producing. Through these one must sustain oneself by what one has put away, or by what others have put away, without which the winters can be long and hard and hungry. And naturally, human nature being what it is, there will always be those who neglect to put in their time in the garden of life and thus who can harvest nothing and store nothing over the winter, and these will be those who seek to take away your squash, your apples, your onions. This is why I am careful to lock up the house and leave the lights and radio on every time we go out, giving the robbers the impression the house is filled with people having a good time. For you must learn that in this life there are people who regard another man's house as their garden, having failed to cultivate their own, for all the various reasons that can never be excused.

15 🦢 Waiting.

It is possible that you have glimpsed me planting seeds in the garden and have wondered why they did not come up at once—and by the same token you may have seen things come up in the garden during one of your rare visits, the beans breaking the surface like big-eared birds, without remembering having seen me plant them. That intervening time during which one can become bored or impatient or inattentive is known as the waiting period, a thing both unbearable and necessary. For the planting of the seed and then the waiting for it to come up and, when it is up, the waiting for it to flower and set fruit, and then the waiting for the fruit to mature—and yet it does not end there, for one must often wait for the fruit, that is, the vegetable, to cook and be served on a plate at the proper time, lunch or dinner, when it is likely to be gobbled up in a flash—this succulent squash that was not only months in the growing but also centuries or even millennia in the developing and perfecting: here it is, swallowed down in a thoughtless gulp. Surely there must be a better arrangement, you remark—or will, when you are old enough. Yet I know of none. For should I be able to plant my seeds in the garden one moment, for example, and be able to watch them sprout and push through the crust of earth the next moment and grow suddenly large and flower and fruit and ripen and bloat, leaves turn yellow, wither, collapse, all within some three or four minutes—so that when I wanted squash, say, or beans or lettuce, I merely walked down to the garden and threw a seed into the ground and stepped back and waited a few minutes for the result, as one waits for toast to emerge from the toaster or water to boil on the stove, then it might well follow that you too would be subject to the same or a similarly accelerated process. For as I plant seeds in the garden and wait for them to germinate and grow and their fruit mature, so too have you been planted in the garden of life and are being watched over by someone who may also wonder why the process is so slow and involves so much waiting—and so on. And yet from your point of view you are likely to feel a little pressed for time—as does perhaps the squash plant, who lies there on the ground pumping and straining away to produce a squash large enough for my plate and my meal, and all the time wishing it had another week or two of hot weather to get the thing out.

But you would do well to consider that the longer and heavier seems the waiting, the more vivid becomes the imagination; that is, those without imagination do not wait so much as simply sit staring vacantly into space. And loss of imagination falls upon those who have harvested too early and too heavily from the garden of desires and who have thereby depleted the soil of nutrients, making subsequent sowings and plantings yield less and less, rather than more and more, and upon those who are not careful to replenish the earth with cover crops, manure, and trace minerals. And it falls equally upon those who, for various reasons, dismiss the garden of desires as an illusion or as an evil and who refuse to patronize it or claim to refuse to patronize it, thus letting it grow wild and become overgrown with weeds, thistles, barbs, stickers, and even cactus.

16 ✽ Pens.

But perhaps you would do better to consider the animals in this connection, for they show impatience only near feeding hours or near term or when the egg is about to be laid or the nest hatch, and who show discomfort only when the snow is deep or when the flies come in swarms in the autumn, and who yet pass their lives in pens behind wire netting, boards, and posts, and who are rarely allowed to venture out—or, in the case of the geese, are allowed to go only as far as the fence lines of the property, and even then only in winter when the garden is dead and the lawns are brown. Certainly they may hanker to explore the willow thickets to the west beyond the barbed wire for nesting sites and may look longingly through the gate at the river across the road and dream of easing their bodies into the swift waters and sailing away forever downstream. But no, they are confined. They have always been. They arrive as goslings in a cardboard box from the feedstore, confined. Yet it is clear that they are not unhappy as they cheep and peck away at the cardboard bottom—indeed, you will notice how contented they seem to be and how they are even a little uneasy when I finally move them into the small wire pen just outside the back door, a pen much more spacious than their cardboard box. Yet they miss the box for a while, with its stiflingly rich aroma, even though they were beginning to bang their heads against its lid. And they are almost in a panic when I carry them in the wire cage down to the large pen in the orchard and set it down and open up one side so they will be able to come and go between their little cage and the large pen. And when autumn comes and I prop open the door to the pen and give them the run of the whole property, you will notice how at first they are always getting their heads stuck or walking into over-turned buckets or tripping over roots—and how for a while, whenever I see them pausing before the fence or the gate and then dipping their necks to pass beneath the lower wire, how I must rush out of the house and wave my arms and hiss until they finally understand and turn back, and again and again, until finally they simply understand.

And as the goslings must be moved from box to cage to pen in accordance with the schedule of their growth, for to move them too rapidly before their feathers are fully developed might result in their falling ill from exposure to cold nights, while keeping them too long in the card-board box or the wire cage might stunt their growth, so too will you find yourself being moved from smaller into larger pens in accordance with a fixed schedule, which at various times will seem too fast or too slow to you, until finally you consider yourself free of all pens and fences and gates and can walk without hindrance down the path of life—which is unending and unbounded, at first appearance. But in time you will make out a fence in the distance, or rather a wall, and it will be only natural for you to change your course in order to avoid it. Yet you will find that it comes up on the horizon again and again on all sides—in exactly the same way that the geese discover after a time that the property, vast as it may have seemed to them at first in comparison with the confines of their pen in the orchard, is bounded on all sides by a strong barbed-wire fence through which they must not pass.

But no doubt at your age, two or three or so, you will find it not only difficult to comprehend all this but impossible to imagine the time when you will finally be able to. But never fear, it will come, even the unimaginable. For as you wax and grow strong and intelligent, so I will wane and grow small and weak in the admirable balance of growth and decline that rules the universe, and some day in the far future you will be able to look down on me as I now look down upon the old gander in the pen, the one who chases you up the garden path and bites your bottom and who seems to rule the flock with an iron rod—but who, if you look closely, does little more than pass the day calling out false alarms at the predators he is the only one to see everywhere in the shadows, in the plum hedges beyond the fence, in the thickets of wild rose and willow down by the road.

17 🦋 Reading and Writing. To

distinguish what is yours from what is another's is an important ability, but unfortunately there is no obvious fixed rule that will cover all cases. What I give to you while saying "This is yours" on whatever occasion, be it birthday or Christmas or at some other time when I am moved by the spirit of generosity, is clearly yours and becomes yours the moment I give it to you, and the same may be said of things that come from others on the same or similar occasions. And from that moment on, you should fix it, the object in question, in your mind as *yours* and not lose track of its whereabouts by leaving it out in the yard, for example, because if I do find it out on the grass it means that you have too many things to keep track of and are failing to keep them put away in your box, on your shelves, or in your closet. As soon as you reach the age of counting, you would do well to number all your toys, from one to fifty, say, or to whatever number equals the grand total, and keep a list of the numbers in a safe place so that now and then you can take an inventory of your possessions, for you will discover soon enough in life that everything has a number and any practice you can get in advance will be invaluable. You might also consider, when you reach the age of writing, making out titles of ownership for each of your toys so that if you decide to trade any of them with a fellow friend, then there will be no question as to its rightful ownership should snags develop in the trading process. This will also enable me to oversee the process more easily and to assure that it is equitable if not profitable from your point of view and to offer you advice concerning subsequent transactions.

What is not yours you should have nothing to do with or as little to do with as possible. For not only are you likely to be held responsible and accountable for whatever you touch that is not yours and thus be subject to recriminations from those who would otherwise have no opportunity to make them, you will also be open to besmirching yourself by handling what is tainted or defective in some way, particularly if you fail to take the sort of precautions you normally would in acquiring an object as your own by purchasing it with money or trading for it with an equivalently valued object. What belongs to other people is theirs usually for good reason, which is, you will soon discover, that it is not up to your exacting standards.

It should begin to be clear to you how important reading and writing are in the garden of life. Now and then you will notice me, if you watch carefully through the cracks in the gate, remove a seed packet from my shirt pocket in order to check whether I planted the seeds at the right depth or to learn when I should begin to thin the seedlings or how long it will be until the first harvest or why the leaves are curling up and turning brown, for the planting of seeds and the cultivation of plants is not a matter of scattering them to the wind and hoping for the best. One must use method. One should follow instructions— within limits. And instructions have been devised by those who know best. Thus the extreme advantage of all those who keep the instructions to the planting of the garden of life in their pockets over those who toss them blithely away and who thrash around in the garden forgetting now one thing, now another, in the belief that paper is only paper. But I will attempt to make this clearer at a later date, for there are many mysteries here. In the meantime it would be of help to you to keep in mind this useful rule, which is that for every object in existence there should exist a corresponding piece of paper—no matter how small, if even just a scrap.

18 ✺ The Allowance. You are too
young yet to receive your allowance—you do not seem to
have yet made the distinction between money and candy
—but at the same time this does not mean that an allowance is not being allowed you, and by that I mean you
have been allotted an allowance although not given it. It
is, in short, going into the bank. Your allowance is that
sum of money I give you each week for performing certain chores which you are not yet in fact performing but
soon will be performing, and alternately it is that sum of
money which I can withhold from you should you will-
fully refuse to perform your chores. Your only chore at the
moment is to grow up to that age at which you can then
carry out your assigned chores, a list of which I have
posted—according to the age at which you are to begin
performing them, plus the allowance you will receive
weekly over the next sixteen years or so—above your bed.
You will notice (eventually) that your allowance began
from the moment it was established that you were con-
ceived, and that it increases by a fixed rate over the years
to a point where, at age eighteen, it will be sufficient to
support you through the first two years of college. It also
features a built-in cost-of-living-change allowance, so that
what are dollars now do not become pennies later and, of
course, your pennies now do not become dollars later.

The use of money is to buy or to save. There is nothing
particularly complicated about this idea, except that you
should note that to buy now is to have no money to buy
later, which is to say that to save now is to have always
the prospect (which is always pleasant) of buying later in
full, clear view—and to save now is in effect to lend
money to others so that they may buy now and so forever

throw away the prospect of buying later—assuming that you cannot both buy and save now. But should you save enough up over the years and decades, then you will have enough to both buy and save at the same time, impossible as this may now seem. Thus, as you receive your weekly allowance, by consulting the charts I have posted above your bed you can determine whether it is worth saving the twenty-five cents a week you now receive or whether it might be better to spend it as soon as received on some small thing that nonetheless may be important to you now —however trivial or flimsy it may seem later on at a time when, for example, you will be receiving five dollars a week (with which you could buy twenty of the above), a sum it will now take you half a year to amass. In other words, to save now and not buy is a slow process at your present age on account of the pittance that is now your allowance, while later it may be easier to save—when your allowance will be large and ample—though your needs and desires may well be correspondingly more developed and awakened. What you must determine now—or soon— or eventually, and the sooner the better—is whether your present desires are larger or smaller than your future desires, in proportion to the sliding scale of your progressively increasing allowance, and this will in turn enable you to determine whether to buy now and save later, or save now and buy later, or attempt to strike a balance by spending a little now and saving a little for later.

I have put aside a set of account books for the time when you will be able to use them, so that you can learn to keep accurate records of when and where and how you spend your allowance over the years. For what would be the point of spending your money thoughtlessly, without learning from each transaction how it might have been better spent or not spent at all, the point, in short, of forgetting about it immediately afterward? For if you develop the habit of spending your money and forgetting about it immediately afterward, then you are likely to lose a clear idea of how much money you have left to spend in the future, and thus will be unable to keep any sort of budget or spending schedule, and so find yourself broke and destitute at an early age—or, worse, in debt to those who do keep careful records of all transactions. Money, as you will eventually learn, has no intrinsic value in itself, being only bits of metal and scraps of paper, and serves only to indicate the wealth or poverty of its owners, that is, the poor man owning little or no money and the rich man owning much, and thus is a barometer or thermometer of a man's inner orderliness or tidiness. Thus, to be rich or poor later on is a decision you yourself will take at a very early age by the manner in which you choose either to husband or to squander your allowance, and the way in which you keep or fail to keep accurate records of all your transactions.

But in no case are you ever to confide in anyone how much money you actually possess, whether it is on your person—and you will be provided with various coin purses and wallets in which to carry money about on you—or in your bank account, for it is important to conceal from your friends at all times how much money you have or, should that be the case, how little you have, and especially when you have no money at all or are deep into debt. You should, in short, no more allow anyone to question you closely about money than to question you about any other matter of personal intimacy. Money should not exist except at the moment of actual transaction, when it surfaces with a flash and a jingle into the light of reality before it slips back into its world of aqueous dream. At your age, or at the age you will soon become, you may believe that there is very little money in the world because you see it so rarely, but the fact of the matter is that there is a great deal of money in the world and that it is everywhere—and everywhere hidden away with great ingeniousness and vigilance. Thus to speak of the money one possesses in cash or in accounts is not unlike taking your money out of your piggy bank or wallet or bank account and spreading it all on the lawn in front of the house or down by the side of the road; it is an act that attracts attention and often results in the loss of all you own amid the arguments and violence of strangers. And, by contrast, admissions of penury and debt are likely to cause those who may have become your friends to flee in more prosperous directions, for there is nothing worse for a person who has a little money than the presence of one who has none at all.

19 🪀 The Sandpile.

In the meantime, however, I suggest that as you play in your sandpile you consider how best to employ its innumerable grains of sand, for though at first appearance a sandpile is a sandpile, it is also a valuable tool or implement which you may use to prepare yourself for your future, work on which can never be begun too early. Indeed it is a well-known fact that the first two years of life are the most important for the individual. You have now passed them, of course, and are thus entering into the old age of your infancy (though the youth of your Childhood), but if you work hard you will certainly be able to catch up with time lost. Sand is an excellent medium out of which to construct roads not unlike those you will one day travel in your course down the path of life, either out of the sand itself packed firm by the action of your little palms or with the addition of a small quantity of water as drawn from a nearby tap, which will make them even firmer. Here you may push your cars and trucks along and thus acquire a notion of traffic, rights of way, easements, property lines, and so on, and also begin making the distinctions among country, suburb, and city by means of the little blocks of wood from the woodpile I have allowed you to play with, the ones free of nails. Houses, you will soon discover, are easily "constructed" by placing blocks of wood here and there next to your roads and by grouping them around stacks of two or three blocks, that is, the stores and office buildings and schools. Sticks are available everywhere in the yard and can represent telephone poles, power lines, and radio and television towers. You will see then the wisdom of making adequate parking space for your many cars and trucks and of allowing sufficient distances between buildings to enable you to drive from place to place. Thus, with your little city or town built, you may pass your time driving back and forth between school, office, house, and store, or hauling around in your trucks the various small objects which will represent the appliances, machinery, supplies, and food that will have to pass from farm and factory to all the rest, or from all the rest—via your garbage trucks—to the dump. Build a bridge out of strips of lath. Build an orchard out of twigs plucked from a dry bush. Build a vast airport where your planes may land and take off. And after a while, should you run out of space or become bored with it, you should feel free to erase the landscape and start all over again from scratch. After all, your little city is only blocks of wood, sand, and twigs. No doubt many a successful city planner or architect has started just this way, in his sandpile.

But you should also make an attempt to select a good site within your miniature city for your own house, so that when the time finally comes twenty or thirty years from now you will find yourself well prepared by your sandpile experience and will thus be able to avoid the more common mistakes. For at first you will no doubt be inclined to put your house down in some low place, some hollow in the sandpile, huddled among other houses like it, small and simple. You will think what a fine thing it is to live so close to other people like yourself, no more than a stone's throw away. But soon it ought to occur to you that by living close to utter strangers you will have to see them more often than you might like, and that they will be noisy when you would like to sleep, or that they will burn trash or weeds in such a way that the smoke will drift into your open windows, and that their cars and mowers will always remind you of their presence, and that their children will widen holes in your hedges as they take shortcuts across your lawn. Thus, already in your sandpile you will learn the advantages to be had in selecting a site well away from your little town—perhaps not even in the sandpile at all—and all its comings and goings, a place somewhat elevated and with attractive scenic views in all directions and no other houses in sight except at such distances as to render them vague and indistinct, mere gleams or glimmers of light or reflection. It follows that such a site will be quiet as well, its silences broken only by whatever noises you choose to make yourself, and will suffer little or not at all from the effects of impure air, as long as you locate it far enough from highways, railway lines, your airport, and whatever factories and power plants there may be to spew forth the usual pollution. And the size of your site can of course be far greater than anything you might find in your crowded little town, thus allowing you to make your house as sprawling as you wish—with several bedrooms, a large garage, a number of bathrooms, a kitchen or two, patios, lawns, and with a driveway of impressive length. There will even be room for a swimming pool, a tennis court, a modest golf course, with the whole surrounded by a cinder bridle path—so that you may swim, play tennis, golf, or ride horseback in untroubled solitude and not have to worry about waiting in line or paying dues, for example. Yet great prominences for your site—hilltops, mountaintops, high ridges—are to be avoided, either because you will be able to see too much of the agitation of the world or because you and your vast and comfortable house will be too visible to those less fortunate than you, those who thrive on envy and poverty and who will lurk around just outside your fences waiting for you to leave your house unguarded. Thus, the site of your sandpile house, like the site of the house of your future, should not view any unpleasantness any more than it should be exposed to harsh northerly winds or be blocked from the sun during the greater part of the winter. But by the same token, it should not be easily visible to whatever unpleasantness there might be in your town, that is, sources of air and noise pollution or social discontent. And finally it should be of enough size and with enough arable land that should conditions in your little town deteriorate even further you will be able to grow your own food in a pinch, generate your own gas and electricity, draw water from your own wells, so that your contact with the rest of society need only be rare and fleeting.

20 ✌ School.

You will find it most useful in connection with your sandpile projects to note the arrangement of the houses and buildings in the villages and towns you are taken through those times I feel you are ready for additional glimpses of the world and take you for a drive. At this age you should pay particular attention to schools. These you will find easy to recognize by their high fences and playgrounds and rows of classrooms. Within a few years you will be there, one of the many children large and small you see out on the playground, although with all the preparation I will have given you by then, I expect you will find the experience less profitable than most. Yet in order to prepare yourself you would do well to begin spending as much time as you can in the company of the chickens, geese, and goats, which you will soon be doing on a regular basis as you help me feed and water them, scatter the grain, cut the alfalfa, and so on, by which apprenticeship you will gradually become the animals' master, that is, their teacher. By beginning with the lowest "grade," the chickens or rabbits, and moving up over a period of time through the geese and finally to the goats, the most intelligent of all, you will acquire some notion of the principles of education which you will be able to apply later in your schooling—a matter mainly of domesticating the intelligence so that it may yield up a fixed and predictable quantity of eggs, milk, etc., year after year. The idea is simple, for school is little more than a series of cages or pens, each one enclosing a separate species and presided over by an adult human who is in charge of feeding and watering the inhabitants and overseeing their general well-being, starting with the small and undemanding animals and ending with large and complicated animals with voracious appetites—horses and cows. In this sense the rabbits of the farm might be said to represent the rabbits of the school, that is, first graders, while horses and milk cows of the farm can be said to represent the horses and cows of the university system, that is, the holders of doctorate degrees. Our little farm goes only up to goats—the master's degree—but as is well known, goats are easier to take care of than cows even though they give less milk, thus less cheese, less butter, and so on. Thus by learning to care for the animals you will obtain an excellent insight into your future educational experience, and will see not only that one must begin at a low level in order to reach a high one but also that the greater number of your fellow pupils will be contented to remain where they are, with the rabbits, chickens, and geese, that is, among the lower levels.

21 ✎ Houses. In the course of placing the wooden blocks on top of each other or alongside each other to form the shape of your future house, it may occur to you that you will perhaps not be living in it alone, that is, that you will have a Wife and Children living there with you at some point sooner or later, for this is only natural. Yet rather than find a Wife and have the Children and then build the house, you would do better to build the house first and then find the Wife and engender the Children. For if you find the Wife first and then build the house to suit her, or her and you both, you risk designing a house that will suit neither her nor you. But by designing and building the house first, before finding the Wife, you will at least be building a house that suits you yourself and with which therefore you can count on always being contented. You should perhaps consider the house as representing the Marriage, so that building the house first is also building the Marriage first, before meeting the Wife, the wisdom of which should be obvious from the sort of discomfort that can result from moving into a house before it is built. And in the same way you will be able to show your future Wife around your already built house so that both she and you may discover if she finds the views pleasing, the house convenient and comfortable and of sufficient size. And if she finds your house agreeable and to her liking, you may then count on her finding the Marriage agreeable and to her liking later on as your Wife. And by the same token, should she be critical of your house and uncomfortable in it, then you may count on her being critical of your Marriage also, and you would do well at that point to suggest that she look elsewhere. Thus by beginning now to practice building your house out of wooden blocks in your sandpile, you are beginning to build not only the house of reality into which you will eventually move, but your Marriage as well—and thus by several removes which I don't expect you to understand quite yet, you are beginning to build in effect your future Wife herself and, by inference, your future Children themselves, out of nothing more than the grains of sand and scraps of wood I have placed at your disposition outside, next to the garage.

Third

To My Daughter
Concerning the Conduct
of Her Childhood

1 🦋 Red Ants. You must understand that you are not allowed to crawl around on the ground outside because of the insects, and primarily because of the red ants. Fascinating as these creatures may seem at first glance, they are known to bite even the young and tender and the most innocent, particularly when trapped between the folds of fat behind the knee, for example, or elsewhere. A swelling in the crotch results—and you stamp your feet and knead the hem of your little skirt in your fists and fall screaming into the ant pile. Once or twice is enough, I should think, certainly enough for you to remember, and if you find the screen door latched and the latch too high to reach, you should try to remember not only the ants outside but their bites as well, for they are indeed connected one to the other.

2 🐝 **Bees.** But no doubt your unfortunate obsession with red ants will pass in due course. There are many other insects worthy of your attention, and perhaps it might be of some use to point out their existence in advance so as to spare you the shock of the raw encounter and thus enable you to graduate more smoothly onto higher levels, and more quickly as well, for puberty and adolescence and adulthood approach with unimaginable speed these days. Flies, to begin with—but perhaps you have had enough of flies by now. Let them remain where they belong on the windowpane, on the wire screen. No doubt bees are next. These are the middling-size winged creatures with brown and amber stripes on their abdomens, with large eyes and hairy shoulders, that you will see rummaging through the flowers with great speed, one then another, one then another, and so on. You will find them lingering around the fresh sawdust at the woodpile on the warm days of late winter. And also you will see them congregating at certain places on the riverbank, particularly where the springs emerge, on the mossy banks of their little trickles. Charming creatures to be sure, without whom pollination would cease and without whom we would have no honey—yet unfortunately for us they can and do sting. And the sting in turn causes a painful swelling beyond anything you have yet experienced, even from your ants, and I earnestly hope you will be spared the experience.

3 🌿 Germs.

Concerning grasshoppers, worms, sow bugs, and other insects, I have less to offer by way of advice. As you will soon discover, some of these are to be found under rocks or under matted deposits of organic matter or will be found nibbling on the leaves of plants in the garden or elsewhere. There is no reason why you should not associate with them for brief periods in the course of your growing up, as long as you refrain from putting them in your mouth. They carry germs—they are themselves visible germs, so to speak—and can thus cause illness of all sorts. You are perhaps too young to comprehend the distinction, the difference between health and illness, but I will make it clear with an example with which you are more familiar. As an invisible germ can be seen to be an extremely small insect, so too can it be seen to be an extremely small animal, an animal not unlike (for example) the neighbor's black dog, which sometimes brushes right past you and knocks you down. And this is exactly what germs will do—they will knock you down, causing you to fall, that is, to fall ill. To get back on your feet and to stop crying is to resume the state and posture of health. The dog here represents the germ.

4 ❦ Appliances.

As soon as you are able to, it would be wise to begin working also on the distinction between your toys and your Brother's, not necessarily so much in terms of whom they actually belong to as in terms of whom they *should* belong to. I certainly acknowledge, let it be known, that you have the right to play with any toys you can lay your hands on and particularly those your Brother leaves scattered around your room or elsewhere abandoned, for it is impossible to know the thing itself without also knowing, before or after, its opposite; thus to play freely with your Brother's cars and trucks, tanks and pistols, compass and binoculars, is a valid means of knowing your own dolls and dollhouses and the miniature stove, refrigerator, iron and ironing board, washing machine and dryer, that have already been placed in your room, to know them by reflection as it were, by what is not to be. And I am certain that your present aversion to these small-scale appliances is not on account of any innate disposition against them but is solely due to your unfortunate habit of trying to hoist yourself into a standing position by grabbing hold of their fragile tin doors and knobs, causing the appliances to tip over on top of you. For in time I am confident that you will be drawn to them and begin to play with them or rather *play them* in the manner of musical instruments in order to produce not so much beautiful sounds as the images of regular meals and clean clothes, as well as the various gestures and postures of domesticity— opening and closing refrigerator doors, bending over sinks, peering into the windows of ovens and washing machines, sweeping up, serving, putting away. It is well to begin early. The time is short and the task is long. In fact, there is said to be none longer.

5 ✥ Foundations.

Indeed, there is no greater accomplishment in life for either man or woman, but particularly for woman, which is what you will eventually become—not even the great cathedrals or the temples guarding the seas, or the invention of the light bulb or the transistor—that is, there can be no greater accomplishment than that of keeping a house clean and meals served regularly on time for forty or fifty years: for by such regular and seemingly tedious and insignificant gestures carried out a sufficient number of times were the Pyramids built, though by men, not women. Yet the woman's pyramid, although invisible, is equally monumental, however little rewarded with the gasps and long silences of admiration with which the man's is normally greeted—she has instead to accept a dribbling of small thanks over the years often uttered lazily or indifferently or even with hostility at that—yet it is no less real than the one the man who will be your Husband's is or will be. Thus, although you are only two years old or so, but given the monumental nature of the structure you must erect over the years, it would be wise to begin laying the foundations for it as soon as possible, so that when the time comes for you to marry in twenty or thirty years from now, you may point to your foundations and say, "Look, they are laid."

I would be pleased to see you put in a set number of hours—or, to begin with, even minutes—at your little tin stove and sink each day, where you may practice making up invisible menus for your dolls and washing dishes with invisible water. Then after a time you may choose—the sequence is logical—to bake invisible bread, pies, cakes, roasts, potatoes, squash, and so on in your little tin oven, and set these out to cool or to be eaten immediately, with leftovers to be stored in your refrigerator or freezer, though if possible let there be no leftovers at all. Canning and freezing of fresh fruit and vegetables will come a little later when you reach a degree of advancement where you are capable of spending whole days at such tasks without boredom or irritation; and then there is the butter to be churned, the yogurt to be cultured, the cheese to be made, the flour to be ground, the honey extracted, bones boiled down, during the odd idle moment. By thus going through the gestures day in and day out you will gradually acquire a touch so expert that when the time comes for you to move your talents into the kitchen of life, which is full size, and take over, then the various implements, ingredients, and appliances will drop into your hands with a naturalness seemingly instinctual, and the casual observer will know without being told that here is a girl whose invisible foundations are solid indeed.

For it will be in the kitchen of reality that you will construct your invisible pyramid piece by piece, just as you laid the foundations for it in your own room, the room of your Childhood, with your tin toy stove and refrigerator, and it will be in the kitchen that you build it up in the slow, gradual accretion of meal after meal over a period of decades into a monument of no mean size, a towering thing made up of the quarter of a million meals and snacks prepared and served and eaten up and cleared away by and for yourself and your Husband and your two Children and the odd dinner guest, that endless marching army who will troop through your kitchen over the next fifty or sixty years, and whom it will be your duty to feed, one and all, day and night.

6 ✿ The Laundry. And so too would it

be wise to begin as early as possible using your toy washing machine and dryer (and the toy clothesline I have built out in the backyard for your exclusive use) to "wash" the dirt from your doll clothes, for in addition to the pyramid of meals you must train your muscles to build, there is also the pyramid of clothes, both clean and dirty, or rather dirty and then clean—or rather two pyramids, in fact, the one clean and the other dirty, the clean becoming the dirty (the new, the old), the dirty the clean, with the cold, warm, or hot, hand wash or machine wash, spin dry, or line hung. That is, in order to visualize the magnitude of the task ahead of you, you should imagine a pyramid many times the size of the entire house and composed of several million articles of dirty clothing, say, to the left, which by means of the intermediary of your washing machine and dryer becomes a pyramid of equal or slightly larger size of clean clothes to the right, with the same army composed of your future Husband, Children, and house guests resolutely putting on the clean clothes from the right-hand side and marching through mudholes, snowdrifts, and up and down grassy slopes over to the left-hand pyramid, where they take off their soiled garments and toss them onto the pile of the dirty, and so on. This might give you a clear idea—eventually. You will need, in addition, approximately nine tons of detergent in liquid or powder form to accomplish this task, and around forty-two acre-feet of water—an entire dam's worth, in fact. But this of course will be primarily your future Husband's task to provide, in addition to the innumerable kilowatts of electricity costing possibly even millions by then, given the present rates of inflation, and so on this account you should not overly concern yourself other than to pick a man who has the potentiality for becoming a good provider when the time comes, one clearly able to finance the building of your pyramids.

7 ✌ Dolls.
You have not learned the proper use of your dolls, either the large "human" dolls with their complete wardrobes and truly amazing abilities (talk, drink, cry, drain, extrude) or your collection of furry animals, but no doubt you shall soon cease chewing on their hands and feet and stop detaching them and throwing them across the room or stuffing the whole dolls and animals into your refrigerator, oven, or freezer, where they do not belong, and leaving them for dead in the middle of the floor. I am tolerant in this respect and will do my best to hold my forbearance in the face of these abuses until you finally learn your dolls' true purpose. However, a little instruction in this area at this time might not be entirely premature, for as the dolls of your Childhood, so too the dolls of your later life, and I mean by them the people who will populate your existence as a real person.

To begin with, it is important for you to keep them put away when you are not playing with them, either in their little beds or cribs or in the box I have provided especially for that purpose, from which places you may withdraw them whenever you feel the urge to walk them or clasp them to your breast or dress or undress them to wash their clothes, or when deciding to feed or drain them—though making a point of draining them after each feeding—or to perform any of the other motherly functions you will soon be in the process of learning. You are now, I believe, the mistress of around nine dolls large and small in addition to some fourteen bears, kangaroos, chickens, dogs, and cats and other stuffed animals, and as it is now your responsibility to undertake the feeding and dressing and so on of them and of keeping them in their places when not in use, so too will it one day be your responsibility to feed and dress and take out and put away the real people and domestic animals of your no doubt lovely home.

But I would be especially pleased if you would stop stuffing the larger dolls into your tin dollhouse. It bends the walls—this is not good—and the large dolls simply do not belong there. There is a difference in scale here which I realize you may not yet perceive but which can be easily explained. The function of the tin dollhouse, with its up-stairs, downstairs, basement, and attic, and its lightweight plastic furniture in the living room, dining room, bed-rooms, and with its bathroom and kitchen fixtures, is to develop your sense of interior decoration, for by moving the miniature sofas and armchairs and tables around you will readily see that they belong in certain places and not in others. No doubt you have tried or someday will try to move all of the living room furniture into the bathroom or kitchen and all the kitchen cabinets into the attic and the pots and pans into the basement and the dining room furniture into the garage and the automobile into the liv-ing room, and it is well to make such experiments in order to see how entirely out of place these objects and furnish-ings are except when they are back in those rooms and in those places where they belong. And the reason the doll-house is so small—though it is a very large one as doll-houses go—is so that you can easily lift the furniture and move it around from room to room to see where it fits and looks best in order to acquire practice for later on when you must shift about the furniture of life and arrange the rooms of life in accordance with the current ideas of what they should look like. But whereas the furniture of your dollhouse is as light as a feather, enabling you to practice without straining or injuring yourself, by contrast the furniture of life is extremely heavy and must usually be shifted about only after long deliberation and with the help of another, preferably your future Husband, who should be strong enough for such tasks. Thus to arrange your dollhouse now is to spare you great exertions later in the house of life, moving furniture. And as the future furniture of your house may be said to be those appliances or machines designed to cushion the seated or reclining body and so to direct, in a subtle manner, the eyes toward the proper view window or fireplace or television screen—one does not, you will learn, place couches or armchairs facing blank walls—so too may the furniture of life be said to be that which lies in the arrangement of the upholstery that directs one's eyes toward what is to be looked at (in life), namely, the pleasant and the bright.

8 🐚 Trash.

The advanced design of your doll-house, which has been pointed out to your friends' mothers more than to your friends—which you are a little young yet to have, I believe—this advanced design not only features a complete line of miniature detergent and cereal boxes and miniature tin cans and bottles by the hundreds but an enlightened trash classification system as well, consisting of separate bins for trash that burns, plastic trash, organic waste, and recycling bins for clean tin cans, clean aluminum, and clean glass, both colored and clear, and it is my hope that you can begin mastering this apparently complex system—though in reality very simple—as soon as possible. For the arrangement and classification of innumerable types of boxes, bottles, packets, and other containers is at the heart of the ecologically sound Marriage, going hand in hand with efficient trash management so that the bringing in of the various shopping bags and boxes to the house from the supermarket is followed by a regular and methodical going out of or purging out of the house of the appropriate quantities of trash or waste so that there is no buildup of unwanted cartons, bottles and cans and wrappers, which can soon fill up a whole house (if not promptly tended to) and bring all activity within it to a halt, in the same way that constipation of the body can. But it is quite another thing to distinguish between what is trash and what is not trash than it is to distinguish among the types of trash, once the first distinction has been made, especially since the "toy" trash of your doll house set is not real trash—yet is—so much as it is pretend trash, that is, simulated trash, artificial trash, or fake trash. What then is trash (trash-trash)? There is perhaps no easy answer to this question other than to suggest that

what is trash is what is thrown down into a bin of one
sort or another, as compared to what is raised up into a
cupboard or shelf or what is set down on the counter or on
the table or even down on the floor, rather than thrown,
so that trash, thus accumulated, is what is later dumped
either into the fireplace or into the pit at the dump from
the back of the truck, or likewise dumped into the various
bins at the recycling center. But to make this distinction
clear, you might do well to imagine the various trash containers—I believe there are seven separate ones in your
dollhouse set—as a kind of musical instrument upon which
you play, with the correct note being struck only when the
correct piece of trash is thrown into the correct bin, thus
filling the house with the sounds of harmony as compared
to the house where the Husband and the Wife indis-
criminately mix the trash, thus sounding notes of discord
and disharmony. If this is still not clear—and it may not
be, to you—then try to think of your little toy xylophone
set as being also a model of a trash management system
which you will learn to "play" over the years—tunes and
melodies—and even though you may start by randomly
banging on it and making nothing more than just noise,
you should take comfort in the thought that all sound
management practices begin with, as it were, the random
blow.

9 ❧ Shopping.

In this connection you would do well to observe your Mother when she shops in the supermarket, from your little seat in the shopping cart, taking particular care to notice what brands of food and household supplies she selects and why. You will see, for example, that she does not blindly rush up and down the aisles and pick out cans and bottles at random but instead proceeds straight to those which offer the best quality at the lowest price—ignoring the shape of the bottle or package, the color or size of the print on the label, special offers or coupons, sales, and so on—knowing as she does by now that the shape of a bottle is not an ingredient in any rational scheme of cooking or that the flavor of a sauce cannot be improved by the color of a label. And in the same manner you will learn how important it is to scrutinize the list of ingredients carefully and, for those which are unfamiliar to you, to then consult the pocket reference works it is always a good idea to carry along with you, in your purse, for what is the point of looking at a list of ingredients while yet having no idea what in reality they are? But even before this, you should learn in detail about the basic manufacturing and food-processing processes involved in the processing and manufacture of the various foods and household products you intend to buy, as it is a well-known fact that food processors are not required to list all the ingredients on their packages. Thus by studying the various books readily available on the subject, and perhaps with the aid of such notes as you might have taken on points of technical or chemical complexity, you will then be ready to enter the supermarket as one who has prepared not only your eyes but your mind and memory as well to spot fraudulent claims, doctored produce, the filled, the fluffed up, and the watered down well in advance, not to speak of the purely and simply poisonous. For you should always remember that the mistake, the ill-advised purchase, that you let pass once may grow if repeated into a habit that spreads over most of your shopping life and which can thus easily cost you a fortune, your health, your peace of mind, or all three, such is the extraordinary power of the addictive substances nowadays added to most foods by their unscrupulous processors.

10 ✌ Cleaning House.

Now I suspect that it is of great puzzlement to you why your little broom and little mop and little battery-powered vacuum cleaner are too large to use in your little tin dollhouse, since that would seem what they are for, as they are obviously not large enough either to handle the sweeping or vacuuming of the vast desertlike expanses of carpet that cover the living room, dining room, and bedrooms. All this is true. Thus I have suggested—and will continue to do so until you finally grasp the point—that you work on only the small area in front of your tin appliances in order to practice the various housecleaning and housekeeping gestures you will need to learn to know, of sweeping, mopping, vacuuming, and of sponging and wiping down as well as wiping up and dusting and polishing, and not worry about the rest of the house. That time will come in due course. Now the object of all these sweepings and wipings will be apparent to you, that being to keep the house clean at all times, and tidy, and well arranged. But you would do well to think of it as something else besides, as something like a game of hide-and-seek in which you are always "it" and always in search of the dirt, which has fallen into the weave of the carpet or has tried to hide in the corners of the sink counters or even between the tiles or the cracks in the kitchen table, and which you must forever find and scrape out. Dirt is quite often capable of rendering itself invisible—making it "fun" to find—as in the thin films on floors and other surfaces such as bathtubs and sinks, where it builds up in rings or in those smudges around door handles on light-colored doors and in so many other places one is likely to become careless about and not think of until it is too late. But it might almost be better for you to think of it as a kind of treasure that has been hidden somewhere in the house and which you must spend your life attempting to find, rather like the eggs of Easter, to give an example. Thus housekeeping becomes with practice an increasingly efficient method for finding whatever is lost or hidden away in the backs of dresser drawers or under rugs or even in the strainer of the washing machine or in dark and rarely visited corners, but a method in which what is found becomes progressively more trivial —the old coin, the button, the unpaid bill, lint balls—for in truth nothing at all has been hidden away or lost except that most essential of human conditions, which is order. Thus in attempting to find order you will—find it, that is, you will find what is perpetually being lost in this ceaseless raining down of little debris in the house of life, until the distinction between what is lost and what is found begins finally to blur and everything is lost—or found—that is, both, at the same time, simultaneously.

11 ❧ The Husband.

Thus I do not advise you to explore the path of life, unlike your Brother. For yours will be rather to guard over the secret life of the house, which itself can be said to represent the secret life of life itself, hidden away, and it will be better for you to wait in the house, perfecting the arts of housekeeping, for that day when your future Husband will arrive fresh from the path of life in his new car, up the driveway, and climb out and march up to the front door to announce himself with a firm knock. You may of course invite him in—I will stand not far off, or crouch, under the sink, repairing a leaky connection. And as he steps inside the door and gives you a smile, you will do well to look over his features in a general way at first and then to inspect them one by one individually, beginning with his teeth. Are they even, with a good bite, and not discolored by nicotine or from the effects of chewing or inhaling other drugs? His mouth is open—smell his breath. Is there a rank emanation, suggesting a future of gum or tonsil problems? Further, does he respond promptly and directly to your questions, or does he have trouble hearing them or understanding them or otherwise making sense of them, as indicated by the manner in which he answers them, whether confused, evasive, or nonsensical? Does he lie? Does he laugh too quickly without apparent cause? Does he stumble about and fall down? Drunk? Stoned? These and other questions you would do well to ask silently at once in order to begin to know whether this is the young man who deserves you as his Wife and me as his Father-in-law, not to speak of your Mother as Mother-in-law, your Brother as Brother-in-law. There are other questions as well, and though they may seem to touch on matters of only minor or passing interest, their answers can often reveal much more than the heavier and more ponderous questions such as What is truth or Who is God? And by these I mean, look at his ears, for example, and notice whether they are turning color as he talks; listen to his chest to ascertain whether he wheezes (indicating asthma) or suffers from shortness of breath, windiness, or other conditions of the lungs and bronchial tubes. You will be sure to observe his shoulders, whether they are thrown back squarely or are unduly hunched forward, and whether his arms hang squarely and are of equal length. Does his stomach growl? If so, is this a temporary condition resulting from a moment of poor judgment, or is it a chronic or permanent one that will keep you awake at night and embarrass your guests? Are his habits regular? His liver? Kidneys? Are his legs of equal length, like his arms, and stout and well fleshed out, or weak and spindly? Will his loins do the job? Do his feet appear flat? And of his conversation may it be said that he is able to discourse upon foreign and domestic affairs at length without boring his listeners and that he is able to speak articulately of his travels, which ought to be extensive, while yet acknowledging freely the still uncharted regions of his own ignorance? Does he have a trade, a skill, a profession—and preferably all three? Ask to see his diplomas. Has he been previously married or otherwise attached? Children, legitimate, illegitimate? If so, how does he propose to support all of you at once? And so on.

Perhaps you would do better to look at your future Husband not so much as a man but as a horse—the powerful steed whom you will someday mount and on whose back you will dash across the meadows and fields and bound up the sides of the highest mountains: for he must be well saddled and bridled and properly cinched up for you to get the best performance out of him, the greatest speed, the highest leaps—for you to ride and ride (as in a dream) until finally a knee goes or he begins to pant too hard or—as has been known to happen—he simply drops dead beneath you.

12 ❧ The House.

But in the meantime, that is, should he prove acceptable on all counts to you as well as pass such oral and written examinations I may choose to submit him to in the privacy of my study, and the Marriage be made, then it will fall upon you to begin the devotions required of the Wife, and perhaps at this time a rough sketch of what will be expected of you is not entirely out of place. To begin with, you are to treat him as a god (since that is what you assuredly will have got) and listen to his words carefully and even memorize phrases of his on occasion so that he need not repeat himself unnecessarily. And accordingly you should regard his person as an object of veneration and awe and make a particular effort to keep all areas where he may choose to stand or sit or recline clear of the random debris of the household, supposing that there happens to be any; and should he complain of any aches or pains or fevers or be in obvious suffering from wounds sustained in his daily battles with other males, you are to offer him such immediate relief as is at your command, either medicinal or physical—but by the same token you are not to inquire whether he is suffering from aches and pains after he has once announced that they have ceased or has requested that they no longer be asked after, which amounts to the same thing. And I should think it would be well to always prepare his meals at the prescribed hour (for he will no doubt be a man of prescribed hours) whether he is in the house or not, so that you do not lose practice in this important matter—and likewise you should make an attempt to always prepare his clothes and bath at the prescribed hour, whether he is there or not to put them on, there or not to lie in the bath. And of course you are not to burden him any more than you would any other honored person with those trivial matters he cannot possibly resolve (an ugly cloud in the sky, a sick stray cat), while at the same time you are to disclose to him in full detail any of the grosser problems that might threaten the integrity of the household, the value of the property, or the very Marriage itself—or whatever else might require that his wrath rise to its full height, with wings spread wide.

And at some future time well after the date of your Marriage, I will call him aside one evening when I happen to detect more impatience or arrogance toward you than usual, and I will sit him down in my study and put a brandy in his hands and then will say, or at least will suggest, or perhaps only intimate in a way that he will be able to make no sense of at first, that he should treat you a little more like a priestess in her temple and that he should pay a little more attention to your sacrifices and burnt offerings and to your rites of purification which attend birth and death and other passages, including those of circumcision, menstruation, and the lesser rites of the threshold and the fireplace, the cupboard, the sink, the bath; and that he should make more effort to respect the dim lighting and the dripping candles and not complain of the incense-laden air, stuffy though it may seem to him at times, nor laugh at the wailings around the altar stone, nor at the flimsy robes that do not cover breasts, nor at the greased lines around eyes and mouths, the long painted nails, nor at the dancing and shrieks that will carry into the night long after he will have dozed off to sleep.

For the house in which you come to settle, which is also your Marriage, will be the house of your inheritance as well. And like the house you will inherit, a house that existed well before you were born, your Marriage too has existed from that time and before, from a time now lost to memory. As you and your future Husband will join together and enter into the house, so too will you enter into a Marriage long since standing. And the Marriage will stand long after you are gone, and it will be then occupied by your Children—who of course will tear down certain rooms and add others and redecorate the entire house to suit their tastes. They will throw out the old furniture. They will buy new appliances. The changes they will make over the years will finally render the old place unrecognizable. Yet, despite all their efforts, the Marriage house will remain the same, for it will look out upon the same views, with the mountains always to the east, the river always to the south, the bluff with its raw clay flanks to the west. What force on earth could possibly ever change these things?

Fourth
and lastly
To My Wife Concerning Some Final Dispositions

1 ✺ The Marriage. It has been said that

the greatest monument that a Husband and his Wife can jointly leave to the world is their Marriage, for this is what can survive all time in the endless reduplications of it in the Marriages that follow, those of their Children, just as their own Marriage is—or should be—a step closer to perfection than all those that have preceded theirs. Thus the Marriage that has been well and strongly built along the lines laid down by tradition, like the house that houses it, will be one that will survive either the Husband or the Wife and can survive even both—while a Marriage that has been carelessly or shoddily built with cheap materials or has employed untried experimental techniques, or one that has been abandoned through infidelity or divorce, will be more easily subject to the rapacious advances of real estate speculators and thus is one that will find itself bulldozed down, its trees uprooted, and its grounds subdivided into tiny parcels for the crackerboxes of the future, and the perpetuation of the endless misery that only cramped quarters can bring about.

Thus in abandoning the Marriage first, as statistically I am most likely to because of the shorter though more intense life of the male, I will do so with the confidence of one who knows he is leaving behind an object built of the finest materials and for which no time or expense has been spared, or will not have been spared by the time I am finished with it thirty or forty years from now, and which will be able by then to carry on without me and my ceaseless efforts—that it will live free-floating though solid, diffuse and cloudlike though intangible to the touch, that it will so surround you and be so ever-present that you will be unlikely to notice even my absence, or will not notice it for long, so everywhere present will I continue to be in that which will always survive, the Marriage which is ours.

Practical considerations, however, have from time to time dictated that I take a more detailed interest in this future event, however improbable it may seem to either you or me at the present moment. I have often observed that to prepare for an event is to make it seem natural, while failing to prepare for it is to make it seem, when it finally takes place, entirely unusual and unnatural, and thus correspondingly more alarming and painful and disruptive. You have noticed yourself, I am sure, how shocking the unexpected fall of an object can be, for example an egg dropped on the kitchen floor, while essentially the same action, that of an egg removed from the refrigerator and carried over to the stove and cracked upon the edge of a frying pan and dropped into the pan, can be the most everyday action in the world and one which is likely to attract no attention at all, and the essential difference between the two, an egg splattering upon a floor, an egg splattering into a frying pan, is that the first is unexpected while the second is not. The second egg, needless to say, remains edible while the first does not, but that is beside the point.

2 ❧ Property. Therefore, in addition to the broad recommendations that are found here, detailed instructions concerning the disposition of my personal property and other matters of importance at that time will be found in that place you will expect to find such things, that is, in the filing cabinet under "D." By that time I will have everything boxed and packed and ready to be distributed to the beneficiaries, and of course each box will be carefully labeled and numbered in accordance with a list that will also be found in the filing cabinet, with each number and the description of the item, as well as the description of the box or carton so itemized, plus the name of the beneficiary to whom it is to be sent or delivered, on the list, though not on the box. The importance of not losing the list should be clear to you, for should you happen to lose the list then it will be impossible to match box to beneficiary. And objects, you must know by now, that is, material possessions, must always be kept in that state of tension known as ownership or propertyhood, for without it they become limp and worthless and thus subject to the abuses of things that are not properly owned, such as neglect, defacement, trampling, dumping, or even malicious ignition—for objects without ownership are like fruits and vegetables which have been pulled from the ground or picked from the tree but which are then left out in the field to shrivel or rot and decay in the sun.

Thus the whole effort of this last transaction should be to effect the transfer of my worldly goods without any delays and gaps such as would contribute to the decay or degradation of the actual property in question. In this connection the list as it now stands refers to some objects I have never owned and do not yet own but which I expect by the end of my life to have owned and to thus own at that actual instant, so that should the moment come to pass a little before or behind schedule you may find items of property on the list which in fact I have never owned or, correspondingly, objects which I have owned that are not yet on the list—minor discrepancies that should cause you no alarm.

In addition I will make every effort to have all accounts, both savings and checking, correctly balanced at the last moment and all household account books brought up to date and closed the day itself, so that the transfer of funds and assets to your name can proceed in a smooth and orderly manner, without loose ends. You will find blank household account and inventory books already set up for the resumption of life in the household along the principles I have laid down, should it in any way resume, the day after, or the day after that.

3 🍂 The Mound. I have elsewhere described in detail arrangements concerning the mound, and all I will add here are a few final—though in this case, preliminary—precautions that have occurred to me in the interim. You should know by now that these arrangements have been meticulously thought through, as usual, and therefore any attempt to alter them in any respect will invalidate the whole and render them all finally impracticable. For example, the measurements I have given for the opening into the walled garden are, with the gates removed, exact down to the inch, and even though the casual observer would say with complete conviction that the opening is too narrow for a small excavating machine to pass through, let alone a dump truck, it will in fact be found that both may do so with ease as long as the driver or drivers are careful and patient and as long as the gates are in fact removed first. They should, of course, be rehung immediately afterward.

The correct procedure for these machines to enter the garden is, in the case of the dump truck, backwards in such a way that its wheels do not stray either to the left or to the right of the twin gravel paths. In other words the driver should not attempt to enter the garden forwards, for in the course of turning his machine around, which he must do in order to dump his load, he will completely flatten most of what is growing there, as well (no doubt) as snagging half of the shrubbery and trees planted around the inside walls with his bumpers and mudguards and so on—or, worse, back into one of the cinder-block walls and knock it down.

The excavating machine must likewise confine itself to the twin gravel paths, likewise entering so as not to have to turn around within the garden itself, and should proceed to the very end of them, that is, to the circular clear space at the exact center of the garden. The garden, as you may remember from your brief visits to it, is divided into four quadrants that converge at this center spot, in order for me to more easily rotate the crops, and at the tip of at least one of these quadrants there will always be a bare space—some years it will be the SW quadrant, some years the NW, and so on—sufficiently large to receive whatever earth must be excavated from the center by the machine, and here, exactly here, and nowhere else, is the dirt to be temporarily put.

I realize it will be extraordinarily tempting for the earth-moving company or crew merely to excavate a corner of the garden for the mound, and for obvious reasons the soil should not be excavated from a site right next to the mound—it will deface the garden—but should be brought instead from a place some distance away, off the property, for a mound standing alone will be pleasant and attractive to look at while a mound next to a pit will tend to slip back into the pit over the years, and will not be pleasing to look at if right next to it—however agreeable a pit may be to look at if found alone, out in the woods, say, or in the middle of a field. You should also take particular care at the proper moment to see that the earth of the mound is properly tamped down into the pleasing mound-like shape I have in mind, even before it is planted with grass and watered, for otherwise the first heavy rain is likely to turn it into something unsightly, such as a low cone of earth, eroded and pebble-strewn, entirely out of place within the confines of the garden.

I specifically request again that you erect no other marker—no brass plaque, no stone, no stake—atop or even near the mound.

4 ✺ **Details.** As you know, I have made no spoken provisions to you concerning final observances—or the lack of same—and it remains for me to add that I have not made written ones either and have no intention of ever doing so. These matters will be entirely in your hands, and you should thus feel free to do nothing at all of a public sort, if that is what you desire, although if you do in fact wish to mark the event in the company of others, whether simply or lavishly, you should feel equally free to do that as well, for it is hardly my place to dictate how you and others should best take note of this or any other passage into nothingness. My own wishes are or will be supremely irrelevant, so that the suggestions that follow should be considered in no way binding or obligatory—and I venture to make them only because a gap here in this critical area may seem somewhat conspicuous to you, given the abundance and richness of my other instructions.

It should be clear to you, for example, that I would not wish you to encourage or even permit religious demonstrations of any kind, knowing as you do that in the course of my life I have not been—and surely will not be—granted visions or other manifestations that might indicate that anything could exist beyond what I happen to have looked at with my eyes or laid my hand upon in the course of time.

By the same token, more or less, I would rather see substituted for the piousness of cut flowers a branch or a bough from an indigenous tree or shrub, or a fresh vegetable recently picked or pulled—or purchased locally, should all this have to take place in winter, and should you choose to invite a few friends in addition to the immediate family. It might not be out of place to remind you here of my fondness for garlic as well as for various greens—yet those who wish to bring fresh fruit should not be discouraged from doing so.

I have not given much thought as to whether the animals ought to be present—another detail whose ultimate decision must rest in your hands. Certainly they would add a pastoral touch in the garden and provide a nice balance to the human element—and point up a too often neglected fact of the dependency of the one upon the other and vice versa—we upon them for eggs and milk, they upon us for grain and hay. You should not of course expect the goats to stand there reverently, less so the geese and the chickens, and in the case of the goats you should make arrangements to prevent them from trampling the garden or nibbling at the vegetation the guests may be carrying, some of which may be poisonous to them. In this connection you might do well to look into hiring a local veterinarian to tranquilize or otherwise pacify the animals so that they may be easily moved the short distance from their pens to inside the walled garden and arranged around the site in a pleasing manner, a half-circle, say, so as to face the other guests and vice versa, crèche-like, if anything. Yet you should make certain that the veterinarian does not over-tranquilize the creatures to the point of making them appear lifeless and dead, that he should strive instead to give them doses that will keep them essentially motionless on their feet, or nearly so. Afterward you should not neglect to lead the animals back to their pens, at which time you might give them a double ration of alfalfa and grain to help them recover from the ordeal.

5 ❧ The Receptacle.

There is, however, one detail I have already tended to. You will only have to arrange for it to be removed from the attic of the garage, where it is now stored under an old canvas. Perhaps I should add at this point that its design—my own—is a little unusual, or will be found unusual by most people, and so perhaps I would do well to advise you in advance not to take offense on my behalf at any adverse criticism that might come within your hearing. Likewise it will undoubtedly be "interpreted" in a variety of ways—as a giant zucchini squash or cucumber or even pea pod—but it should also be obvious that I have nothing specific in mind except a somewhat organic podlike shape whose advantages ought soon to be apparent to all present, for not only does its shape render it far stronger than conventional designs, it also makes the whole far lighter and thus easier to carry and lower without unsightly winches and other machinery. Care, however, must be taken not to damage its fiberglass shell, and you should make a point of seeing that the somewhat complicated latches are properly opened and closed at the appropriate times. They are push-button and pin affairs: to open you push the button and pull out the pin, whereupon you can split open the two halves of the shell, and to close them up you reverse the process. But the difficulty here is in passing each pin through each of the four holes necessary to secure the lid back in place. Above all, you—or whoever is doing this—should not attempt to drive the pins back in with a screwdriver and hammer, as this is likely to completely pull out the latch rivets from the green fiberglass hull or shell and thus generally ruin the appearance of the whole, which will then have to

be roped or wired or strapped closed before being lowered
into the earth.

6 ❧ **Observances.** The rest—and there is much—I leave entirely in your hands, though in closing it occurs to me that the question of the length of the period of mourning is bound to arise in a way that no one can settle in a satisfactory manner except myself, who must remain silent at that time. When it is to begin should be clear enough, but when it is to end is another matter altogether; however, I would suggest in advance that in keeping with the fast-moving spirit of the times—and the even faster-moving spirit of the times to come—to which even I must finally submit, it should not exceed the length of the very day the rites are performed and should end with the fall of night of that day, and thus will vary according to the season, short in winter, long in summer, and of medium length spring and autumn. This will be an amount of time brief enough to be easily spanned with an appropriate intensity in comparison with the more traditional and long-drawn-out and progressively more irksome period of mourning. Yet should this time seem to you too brief you may choose to heighten its dramatic effect, as it were, by requesting the inhabitants of the neighborhood to refrain from driving their cars, firing off their guns, using their chain saws, mowers, tillers, and tractors during the day in question, and request also that schools, stores, and the post office close down in the village. In this way the final silence of the garden and of the house and Marriage will find echo throughout the valley, and one day should easily be sufficient.

The Marriage
❧ Almanac ❧

I HAVE PREPARED THE SEASONAL CAL-
endar below for the use of the joint partners of the Marriage,
that is, you and I, for reasons explained elsewhere (I.6). I intend
it only as a rough guide, as based on the accumulated experience
of our Marriage. The more detailed eating, dressing, bathing, and
other schedules, most of which will not be affected by whatever
inaccuracies there may be found in this larger and more sweeping view of the years to come, are located in those places which
by now you know well enough, as posted inside the appropriate
cupboard and closet doors. Yet should none of the problems that
I anticipate below come to pass in any one year, nothing in effect
will have been wasted except the anticipation itself, and in most
cases it will be found to be only premature. You should not take,
in short, this Almanac as definitive for any particular year but as
definitive only in a larger sense to be revealed over the course of
several more—perhaps even many more—years—decades.

Winter ❀

.⸳◦⸳◦⸳◦⸳◦⸳◦⸳◦⸳◦⸳◦⸳◦⸳◦⸳◦⸳◦⸳◦⸳◦⸳◦.

DECEMBER 23–MARCH 22
DRESSING SCHEDULE "A," MENU AND
MEAL HOURS SCHEDULE "A," SLEEPING
AND NAP SCHEDULE "A," BATHING
SCHEDULE "A," SHOPPING SCHEDULE
"A," ENTERTAINMENT SCHEDULE "A,"
CONJUGAL RELATIONS SCHEDULE "A"

1 ❀ The great threat of the season is not the coldness but the dryness of the air or the lowness of the humidity, which can render the skin dry and flaky and irritate the passages of the sinuses, throat, and bronchial tubes. Therefore you should make an effort to keep your body well oiled and lotioned and to put out pans of water to simmer on the stove at all times in order to keep the humidity of the house up, thus avoiding sore throats and colds. A moist throat means a clear voice and a nose that needs to be but rarely blown, and discreetly at that, and thus the Marriage will be free of unseemly coughs, sneezes, loud and extended throat clearings, garglings, and spittings that only serve to spread the conditions that could have been so easily avoided at the first signs of low humidity—the runny nose and the hoarse voice.

2 ❀ As dryness is but one extreme of wetness, being the total absence of moisture, so too is freezing the other and opposite extreme, that of moisture arrested into ice. And as with the nasal and bronchial passages of the members of the household, so too with the pipes of the house itself, and particularly the water pipes, which must be observed with equal care so that they do not become too "dry" and thus catch cold, as it were, and freeze up and burst in the basement of the house. For this reason during the coldest periods of January, the clear nights that follow snowstorms, the taps should be left dribbling in the kitchen and in the bathroom overnight in order to keep the water circulating in a gentle way throughout the various pipes under the house so that you or I, or both, do not wake up on cold mornings and find them frozen and no water flowing from them—in short, dry, having caught severely "cold." For a house without water in the winter is like a nasal passage that is swollen and inflamed and through which air passes with difficulty or not at all, and the effect of both, frozen pipes upon the Marriage, swollen passages upon the nose, is the same or similar, that is, one of great irritation.

3 🐚 You will do well to discourage visitors of all kinds during the more severe weeks of the winter, particularly early January, for most of them will be suffering in various ways from the extremes of temperature and humidity, their houses will be cold, their plumbing ruined or out of order, and their Marriages will be breaking up under the strain or under the effects of the over-indulgence that the strain of the subzero temperatures brings on. By the same token, you should urge the Children to observe the habits of the squirrel and the bear, who hibernate during the winter, so that they will be thereby encouraged to take long naps and go to bed earlier than usual.

Spring 🦋

MARCH 23–JUNE 22

DRESSING SCHEDULE "B," MENU AND
MEAL HOURS SCHEDULE "B," SLEEPING
AND NAP SCHEDULE "B," BATHING
SCHEDULE "B," SHOPPING SCHEDULE
"B," ENTERTAINMENT SCHEDULE "B,"
CONJUGAL RELATIONS SCHEDULE "B"

1 🦋 Early spring is traditionally the time of infection, and thus at the first sign of warm or windy weather, when the germs begin to breed and move about, you should double the family vitamin intake, and begin the Children's daily spring doses of garlic and honey mixed with a little wine and then continue them throughout the spring, depending on the weather and the reports of illness and infection in the neighborhood.

2 🦋 It should be clear that you should make every attempt to discourage callers who are either sick with colds or the flu or any other disease, or who have been recently exposed to anything at all contagious, as most diseases obviously must be. Yet those friends who seem to be in perfect health are the ones precisely to be the most avoided, for their colds and flu are no doubt in the gestation stage, which is the most contagious of all. Thus you will see that the best course is to invite in only those who are recovering from their ailments, a time of "grace" when it is impossible to catch anything new and therefore impossible to pass it on. For similar reasons Shopping Schedule "B" shifts our shopping excursions to the early morning hours, a time when the sick are still lying in bed and the air has not been filled up with germs, and the fresh produce has not yet been worked over by infected hands.

3 🦋 The positive value of illness must not be overlooked, however, should either you or I, the joint partners of the Marriage,

fall prey to the bacteria, viruses, or fungi that float through the air in no doubt dense clouds at this time of year. Illness is what renders palpable or visible what has been invisible or insidious beforehand, for the body stands to the germ as the earth to the seed, so that when the germ falls upon the body and sends down roots and sends up shoots, and so grows, flowers, and fruits into aches and pains, fevers and swellings, rashes and lumps, you would do well to consider that this is what the very earth feels at the coming of spring, and that like the earth itself the only course for the body is to lie still and uncomplaining while drinking lots of liquid (to be likened to the rains of spring) until such time as the course of the disease passes into autumn and winter, and finally withers and dies.

4 🦋 And as you know, the first effusions of spring upon being translated into human exuberance can often result in serious accidents, and you will do well to be more careful at this time of year than at any other. The weather, as always, plays an important part in the life of the body, which is particularly subject to the alternations of wetness and dryness, heat and cold, windiness and stillness, cloudiness and clearness, rises and falls in pressure, in addition to the usual effects of darkness and light, of night and day. Under these endlessly changing conditions you are to be particularly alert while handling knives and hammers, and to avoid opening or closing doors or windows precipitously for any reason at all. Watch also heavy objects that you may wish to carry from place to place so that you do not drop them on your feet, and do not light fires inside or outside unless you have in advance a clear notion of how to put them out. You would be wise to have a fire extinguisher and first-aid kit within reach at all times during the most changeable weeks of spring, if in fact you are unable to carry them around with you. The Children should not be allowed to put any object in their mouths until it has been thoroughly inspected, and should not be given anything that could possibly become lodged in their throats (and above all, not at the same time), and you should not let them out of your

sight unless it is for them to go to a fixed destination for a pre-determined time, such as to and from the bathroom.

5 🐝 It is my conviction that the function of the spring cleaning, which should take place in late May, is primarily to prevent the accumulation of pollens within the house, as I have (I believe) occasionally attempted to explain. For should the pollens as carried by the late spring winds across the fields and as they settle down into the house, passing through the windows open for the first time in months, and through the wire mesh of the newly rehung screen doors—to swirl around inside the rooms of the house and collect in little eddies behind the chairs and sofas—should these invisible pollen clouds be left to lie where they form and gather, then each time you or I walk through the house or sit down in a chair a great cloud of these invisible particles will jump to life and fill the air and cause our noses to run or to sneeze, our lungs to fill up, eyes to water. A house clogged with pollens is a Marriage that lives muffled under a blanket of hay fever and thus is one in which the finer sensations cannot be perceived through the blocked and stuffed-up senses on the one hand or through the debilitating effects of the powerful drugs that alleviate the symptoms on the other. To prevent the buildup of pollens in the house is thus to prevent it in the Marriage as well, enabling the Husband and the Wife to breathe without wheezing, speak without sniffling, see without watery eyes, and taste within the full range of the palate. You may wish to see the pollens as representing all that which is blowing in from afar that might have an essentially irritating effect upon either you or myself, the joint partners of the Marriage, and thus upon the Marriage as a whole.

Summer 🦋

JUNE 23–SEPTEMBER 22
DRESSING SCHEDULE "C," MENU AND
MEAL HOURS SCHEDULE "C," SLEEPING
AND NAP SCHEDULE "C," BATHING
SCHEDULE "C," SHOPPING SCHEDULE
"C," ENTERTAINMENT SCHEDULE "C,"
CONJUGAL RELATIONS SCHEDULE "C"

1 🦋 At the outset of the summer you are to conduct the annual poisonous weed and plant tour of the neighborhood for the benefit of the Children, who will sooner or later, by repeated exposure, come to know well what they are not to eat or to touch. By the same token, however, you are not to point out which weeds or plants might be edible in a pinch, for it is more important at this time in their lives to suggest that *all* plants or weeds that have not been deliberately planted by myself within the walled garden or elsewhere in the yard are essentially dangerous to eat, that is, poisonous, particularly *all* mushrooms, which you should make a point of always calling toadstools, at least for the time being, except those that are purchased from the local supermarket, whether canned or fresh.

2 🦋 I need not point out the value of preserving the various fruits and vegetables grown within the garden by any of the various means such as canning (hot- or cold-pack method), freezing, drying, or by storage in the root cellar or elsewhere, for it would seem obvious by now that in order to eat in the winter when the snow is piled high on the earth it is necessary to prepare somewhat in advance, usually from around midsummer to early autumn. And preserving in the summer in order to eat throughout the winter involves all those utensils and implements with which you are now familiar, including pressure cookers and canners, blanchers, canning jars, lids and rings, cooling racks, ice-water dips, freezer containers and lids, labels, and so on. In many ways the true wealth of a Marriage may be best measured not by how much money is held by the Husband and the Wife in their various accounts, individual or joint, or in stocks and bonds, but in how many jars of peaches, plums, apricots, and various jams have been canned and put away in the pantry, or how many containers of peas and beans have been frozen, how many pounds of pumpkin and squash put away, pounds of onions hung, bulbs of garlic, bushels of apples, bags of nuts, sacks of potatoes, flats of chicory, sacks of grain, and so on, for it will be the strong and confident Marriage that lays in a full year's supply, in addition to emergency rations, secure in the knowledge that Husband and Wife will remain Husband and Wife throughout the winter—while it is a weak and shaky Marriage that lets the summer pass without canning or freezing or drying and makes a feeble effort to save a few tomatoes and pumpkins the night of the first frost, food sufficient for only a day or two or a week at best.

Thus to keep in good repair the various tools and implements of canning and freezing is to keep in good repair the future of the Marriage itself, and you should make every effort to wash carefully and inspect closely the various canning jars and freezer containers as soon as they have been emptied, and to store them in a clean dust-free place against the time when they will next be used. Canning and freezing thus is not something that takes place only from late June through September but is something that you must do throughout the entire course of the year, just as the future of the Marriage must always be cared for in the present and never allowed to go to neglect. To make this clear you should visualize the Marriage as the canning jar or freezer container which, year after year, must be reused. That which is yearly poured into it, the freshly cooked or blanched fruit or vegetable, and from which all take sustenance, Husband, Wife, and Children, is the present state of the Marriage as renewed year after year.

Autumn 🌾

SEPTEMBER 23–DECEMBER 22
DRESSING SCHEDULE "D," MENU AND
MEAL HOURS SCHEDULE "D," SLEEPING
AND NAP SCHEDULE "D," BATHING
SCHEDULE "D," SHOPPING SCHEDULE
"D," ENTERTAINMENT SCHEDULE "D,"
CONJUGAL RELATIONS SCHEDULE "D"

I have taken it upon myself to tend those plants, bushes, shrubs, and trees which provide us with the greater part of our fruits and vegetables over much of the year, and from which it is up to you to select those that are fit for our table or for storage and to cull out those that are unfit. This is particularly important during the early weeks of the month of October when putting away squash, apples, onions, winter pears, cabbages, and carrots for overwinter storage, for it is a well-known fact that if the fit and the unfit, the good and the bad, the whole and the rotten, are mixed together, the end result in a few months will be an increased quantity of the unfit, the bad, and the rotten, and a decreased quantity of the fit, the good, and the whole—if not their complete extinction. Thus as you select fruits and vegetables for storage, you must pay particular attention to any bruises, cuts, holes, slashes, or openings that might result in the gradual destruction of the whole fruit or vegetable and, from there, the destruction of its immediate neighbors, and so on, until the whole storage bin, box, or bag has been affected. Thus to correctly sort and store at this time is to be assured of a regular supply of fresh fruit and vegetables later on, of undiminished succulence and flavor.

Food, it has been said, is the only true and reliable friend of man, an undeniable comfort from childhood to old age, and by the same token you should choose your friends for their storing and keeping qualities above all others, particularly at the end of autumn or at the beginning of winter. And like squash, apples, onions, and potatoes, they should be fully matured, well ripened by natural processes, and free of external blemishes—that is, in the case of friends, should be good-natured and cheerful and not likely to go soft or rotten prematurely. True, these qualities are rare if not nonexistent at the present time—we live among lettuces, spinach, radishes, and other forty-five-day wonders, all quick to bolt in hot weather and with no tolerance for frost at all.

✿ Index ✿

tools, 66–68
  injury to, 67
  loss of, 66
toys, 120
  childhood, 79, 81
  distinguishing ownership,
    99
  playing with, 74–75
  putting away, 74–76, 81
  worse and better, 87
trash
  artificial, 129
  containers, 9
  management systems, 129–
    130
  and non-trash, 80, 129–130
treasure, 134
truth, What is?, 136

U

the unimaginable, 98
unseemly coughs, 159
unsightly winches, 152
upholstery, 128

V

vegetarians, 54
veterinarians, 151
violence of strangers, 105
viruses, 162
visions, 150
visiting others, 69–70

visitors
  casual, 91
  visiting times, 61
vows, 35–36

W

wagon, 83
waiting period, 94
walls
  garden, 57, 92, 147
  house, 26
washing machine, 120, 124
water, invisible, 122
water pipes, 159
weather, 40–41, 82
weeds, 57–58
Wife, 135, 143, 163
  devotions of, 138
  future, 112–113
  speaking at meals, 53
windiness, 136
windows, 32, 37, 38
world, the, 110
worldly goods, 145–146

X

xylophone, 130

Y

yard
  condition of, 33
  as courtship, 21